Mud On Her Boots

Corene Trevelyn Johnston

Copyright © 2015 by Corene Trevelyn Johnston

All rights reserved. This book or any portion thereof may not be reproduced or used in any manner whatsoever without the expressed written permission of the publisher.

Published by Blue Blaze Books
Newark, DE 19711

First printing 2015

ISBN 978-0-9913288-9-5

Editor: Georgiana Johnson
Creative Designer: Rebecca L. Taccone
Contributors: Bibiana Polak and Teresa Stouffer

Forget not that the earth delights to feel your bare feet and the winds long to play with your hair.

— Khalil Gibran

Gossip

Golden aspens chatter with the news;
pines sigh in stage whispers:
the end of autumn is near.

Oh yes,
once today's rain ceases weeping,
there will be a few more days of Indian Summer;
to sit warm upon crackling leaves,
to press against the sun,
and watch the Earth undress for sleep.

But then will come the pewter cold.
And the pines, whispering now around their cones,
will become responsible
for the keeping of the green
through the long, leafless winter.

Worn Through

Don't speak to me of things too real,
for I am your mother.
Tell me what you do,
not how you feel.

Write to me
that you have bought a new car,
that your child's hair is red,
that you have a new job.

Do not tell me
that driving fast brings you close to orgasm,
that you sometimes hate your red-haired child
for being simply that – your child;
that keeping one job too long
would cause you to slow
and deaden inside.

I will tell you what I think,
how I expect you to behave,
that I am proud of your writing,
ashamed of your divorce;
for I can deal with expectation,
with pride and shame for you.

Do not ask me how I feel.
I do not want to feel.

I do not want to remember when,
before I allowed it to fatten
and protect me from such yearning,
my body was as beautiful and my hair as shining as yours,
and I would wonder who would touch and appreciate.

I do not want to remember
when I still had dreams,
for awakening from them hurt
far more than the headaches
which have replaced them.

Do not ask me what I feel,
for I have learned not to,
and if now
you must feel and live for us both,
knowing the roots
of your exhilarations and agonies,
so full now, of the juices of life,
are sprouted from mine,
so dry now, desiccated nearly to sawdust,
well then,
we shall just not talk about it.

It has been snowing here,
and we took the dog in for his shots today.

Three Days

I didn't want the curtains open
for three days after I had surgery.

 "The light hurts my eyes," I said,
"it must be from the anesthesia."
The light did hurt my eyes.
And it probably was caused by the potions of toxic sleep.
But that's not why I left the room in shadow.

With the draperies drawn,
and the door closed upon a hall noisy with food carts,
and worried families, and yellow-skinned dying people pacing,
I spend three days alone, inside my head.

Three days
without choking off tears to end an unresolved argument,
with no laundry to do, no meal to cook,
no decision to make for another.

On the tan wall at the foot of my bed,
I could watch my own thoughts.

The price was cheap.
All I had to do to have three days alone
in a room with the curtains closed,
was to get cancer.

Saturday Morning

Saturday morning
she walked downtown
in levis,
and fat, hollow,
pink rollers wrapped with damp strands
of dark hair,
covered by a transparent
blue nylon scarf.

Tonight would be a movie
at the drive-in,
but now was printed birthday napkins
from the dime store,
and masking tape
from the hardware.

On the way home,
she did not turn her head
much
in front of the Sunoco station,
where the boys in blue coveralls
and fingernail grease
stopped pumping gas
and shooting bull
to watch the tight-stretched denim
so awarely grinding past.

A Gift of Time

My mind ricochets off the dreams of you.
Why won't you remain a fantasy?
Or,
why must the fantasy remain one?
Which of these do I ask?

My mind must dwell in reality,
but my soul reaches out for ecstasy –
the ecstasy of you.
But that, of course, is ecstasy only because
it is fantasy.
(Or is it?)

My mind must dwell in reality.

My mind ricochets off the dreams of you.
I cannot distinguish,
sometimes,
between
dreams
and plans.

Between
mind
and soul.

Sachet

A smile slips into my eyes
as softly
as a long unworn drift of silken lingerie,
stored in the scented dark of a bureau drawer,
until the joy of reawakened senses
calls forth its memory.

Then,
like dried rose petals dropping
from folds once more whispering
against warm flesh,
a few tears fall.

Big toe sandal smile
free at last
for summer grass and gravel

Eclipse

Roundness comforts me.
Roundness is woman.
Roundness is nurture.

Straight the artificial lines of men:
furrows, sidewalks, pillars;
fragile interesting things, but not stable.

Nature's architecture is curvilinear.
Light, sound, thought, eternity
project straight forth
in paths that circle the cosmos,
then spiral back, complete, from whence they came.

In curves we feel balance, comfort, and a satisfying lust.
The silver cycles of the moon.
The sexy bulge of a pregnant belly.
The sun, my totem, caricatured into a smiling face.
The belly dance I did on an old man's birthday.
The juice-taut skin of a cinnamon colored grape.

The circle of seasons.
The eternal helix of our repeating genes.
The wide, trusting eyes of babies –
vulpine, human, fervid, feline – all babies.
The veined, oval vessel of a nursing woman's breast.
The curve of my own breast beneath a smooth, black leotard.

But now, inside of me,
inside the roundness of my breast,
grows another roundness;
hard,
smaller than a marble, a child's toy, tinier even than that!
A roundness that will make me die.

Starting with my breast,
it will send its children forth
eating,
spreading,
sucking the thoughts from my brain,
the air from my lungs,
the proud, pearly hardness from my bones.

I will die
unless I tell someone
to cut it out of me;
to cut out a piece of the soft, round flesh,
pink as laurel blossoms,
that swells to the lips of a lover,
that hardens
when there is a solid, wanting cock
in the warm, wet hugging space between my thighs.
Perhaps I should tell someone in white
all nice and tidy,
to cut it all off, the soft, rose-tipped pleasure giving part of me
that holds a death marble,
and fill the empty space with plastic.

Tenuous Tenderness

I have not been gentle
for so long,
but today I rediscovered Richard Brautigan,
and now I can be gentle again.

I can be as gentle
as an oyster putting on suntan oil,
which is Brautigan's kind of gentle.

Or, I can be as gentle
as not yelling at Jack,
which is my kind of gentle.

But this gentleness may last only for tonight,
because my transmission is falling out,
and I have no money,
and other assorted reasons
for having to slog through the mucus of life,
which somehow,
viscously,
dissolves gentleness
and leaves a gritty sediment
of bilious survival.

Kernels

This day has been an exercise
in futile activity
So I have ceased to rail
at the frustration of life.
I submit.
I succumb.
I sink into the formless mud
at the bottom of unnamed existence.

Slowly,
I slog to the top of the steep back yard,
then return, hands full,
to the kitchen where a kettle is just beginning to boil.

In ten minutes,
milky juice squirts between my teeth,
from the garden's turgid first ear of corn,
buttered,
and salted.

Life seems,
again,
a journey with a destination.
I laugh
and continue.

Night Song

Your eyelash winks in the dusky, lilac sky.
Our lunar flirtation begins.
And with your silver light, you make us beautiful as you,
Oh darling of our night,
Sister Moon.

Your gravid belly grows amid quartzy stars
Maternal, you peek into our dreams.
Sing us a silver lullaby, as beautiful as you,
Oh guardian of our night,
Mother Moon.

Your slowly shrinking crescent stays up to greet the sun.
From you we learn there's beauty in each phase.
Bid us a silver farewell, as beautiful as you,
Oh teacher of our night,
Grandmother Moon.

Someday

Someday there'll be a time, My dear,
when our hands get thin,
and the veins stand out bluish grey,
under the loose brown skin,
And the knuckles are like burls in the trunks of thin gingers.

Someday I'll watch
the loose folds of your neck,
above a shirt open at the collar,
frayed and out of style
and beloved.

Someday, a man will remember these dishes –
by then cracked and mostly broken,
from long ago when he was a child.

Someday, the feel of my slack flesh
beside you under a sheet
will give you a contented familiar warmth
to equal the fire in your fingers
now caressing the curves of my firm, tan skin.

Someday, this band will be worn to narrow fragility
but the light will catch the glints of golden reflections
on its smooth curved surface.

Santa Ana Fires

The flames in southern California are nearly smothered,
Flames that have roared and snapped
their ashy, melted plastic way
Through the anthill dense condos of San Diego.

No longer are the wildfires limited to the forests that need them,
With losses only to the very rich and very poor,
Scattered at scant, hunter-gatherer density
In places that support renewing cycles.
Now the fires clear settlements,
which humans expect to be the same,
always,
no end and no renewal.

With their mothers and their fathers,
their aunts and uncles and Grandpas,
I helped pray one small family through:
a mother,
a father,
a baby,
a dog named Chubby.

They were unharmed.
Theirs was a condo that did not burn.

The Ballet

The gluteal muscles,
the quadriceps,
abdominus rectus,
trapezius,
trained and hard,
relax and tighten
beneath sweat-shining skin.

Swans and sylphs in white organdy
glide,
without effort,
through a magic forest.

Behind stage,
the floor is littered with sweatpants and socks.
The choreographer swears softly, and paces.

411, Please

Oh Ma,
It's been twelve years, almost,
and still,
I awaken thinking to carry my coffee to my kitchen desk,
and drink it on the phone with you.

Not the little bird of you,
all that was left at the end,
but the real you.

You know,
the you I used to address as "Maaaaaahhhm!"
despairing at the archaic density of your adulthood.

The you I called in tears,
one midnight,
from my dorm,
because my boyfriend was gonna dump me,
if I didn't go to bed with him.

I need to call you right now, Ma,
and tell you I'm a married widow.
My husband had a stroke and is paralyzed.
Mama, he's in a nursing home.

Mama, I need to talk to you.

And to tell you about Domino, the kitten.
The one I brought back from Michigan.

You don't know, yet,
that it cost me eighty bucks to bring him on the plane.

He's already 12 or 13 pounds,
and he walks around
with a big chicken feather sticking out both sides of his mouth.
Ma, he just carries it around like a trophy.

Fix yourself a cup of tea, Mom, I'm about to call.

Even now,
after twelve years, almost,
I start to reach for the phone.

But Ma, I don't know your number in heaven.

Abeth

Aghast,
I stare out the front window.
Her ballerina foreleg
dangles from her shoulder,
so mutilated
it hardly seems possible it could have been grown
from that graceful grey brown body.
And the fur,
great gaps of it gone from her side,
exposing raw, red skin.
She bends her neck to seek a frozen acorn
beneath the skiff of snow on our grass.

Could this be the doe to whom I sang,
in the heady, sherry light of autumn,
as she browsed with her yearling son,
and I shepherded my goats,
in the second-growth forest
that is her address, and mine?

Hunting season is six weeks past.
No young buck attends her now.
She hobbles alone through the grey of winter.
I put goat food on the picnic table
and sing as she warily chews,
but I cannot ease the pain.
The healing is hers, alone.

By spring,
the skin has closed.

Her shattered, withered leg has become a crutch.
She has learned that she need not run in panic
from singing humans.

I hope she still knows to fear
the silent ones.

The world turns green, her coat orange,
a lighter tan where the skin and fur are new.

Her absences are longer;
she can browse a wider range.

One morning from his desk,
my husband watches Abeth,
for so I know her name to be,
selecting certain, tender blades of grass, then,
beside her,
a motion…
a spotted fawn!

Through sleety snow and pain,
this mother
harbored a tiny, amber life within her,
and leads it now, into our yard.

On another day,
I nearly stumble over the mottled baby
she has hidden, asleep, in dappled hemlock shelter.

In July, we are given our final anointing,
as we dine on the porch.

Abeth browses her way down the bank, beside our yard,
reaches the open lane,
and out of the gully, bound two spotted babies!
Twins!
Joyfully, they butt and push and nurse.

In our full view,
Abeth stands strong and stable;
nourishing them.

My husband and I, at the porch rail, hold hands.
I sing, softly.

Abeth,
beautiful mother,
crippled but not disabled,
we heed and honor the title of Trusted Neighbor
you bestow upon us.

A Woman of 40 Trying to Conceive

She tries.
She cries
in desperation,
pouring into her body
chemicals made, not within the warm, familiar dark
of her sheltering skull,
or the flared, welcoming bowl of her alabaster pelvis,
but in cold glass,
in a laboratory named Ortho, or Sandoz.

She fills the hormone-purpled mouth of her womb
with sperm of a man who has never breathed upon her skin,
overflowed her mind with realness,
saturated her memory.

Each Moon cycle she tries.
Each Moon cycle she cries,
knowing not that the Moon is her wise Grandmother,
her loving Mother,
her sharing Sister.

Each month, with the unaware self-hatred of an anorexic,
the world-induced hysteria of a bulimic,
she forces her body to submit
to a test of plumbing.

Youth Song

A long lean boy came to our door,
guitar held in his arms.
He said, "I've come to visit,
come to serenade your farm."

I looked at him, then let him in,
and listened while he sang,
and from his strings, and from his lips,
the old truths cleanly rang.

"Let's put an end to killing,
let's sing about our land,
let's cherish love unending"
were the themes beneath his hands.

I watched him sing of mountains
and of love's confusing ways,
and his flashing eyes and fingers
held my fascinated gaze.

He was so young, and such a vision
of sweet invincibility,
such a perfect inspiration
for loin lust and poetry.

Yes, this young man shall have his fill
of life and ladies, too,
then turn them into music
and sing them sweet for you.

When I met his eyes and saw his soul
do a pirouette for me,
I smiled and penned a ballad
'bout loin lust and poetry.

Chronicle

On a windswept beach,
intricate patterns in sand,
carefully traced,
speak of the past…
and vanish.

Alzheimer's

That blue-veined old woman had left, finally;
the one who had so long kept him
from the business
of properly mourning his wife.

That old woman had to be bathed,
each morning,
after lying beside him all night,
her sleeping flesh bitterly parroting
the solid, long-shanked loveliness
of the wife who thrice had swelled
with his seed.

That old woman's sweater had to be buttoned,
after pulling each unprotesting arm through a sleeve,
across breasts that mimed those of his wife,
whose rigid nipples had brought him up,
just as hard,
then suckled the babies
born from their joined,
joyous,
tumescent
flesh.

That old woman had worn diapers,
not the peach-colored, rayon "silkies" of his wife.

Even to bed, his wife had worn them,
on the nights she was bleeding.
And silky they had felt,
as he slipped them from her raised hips, whispering
"Tonight I can really feel you. The blood will make it safe."

Changing the diapers,
buttoning the sweater,
drawing the bath
each day,
for a thousand endless days,
he had left his unfinished business with his wife
waiting.

But the old woman,
that blue-veined old woman,
had needed his care.
And he had given it –
his wife would have understood –
each day, for a thousand endless days.

But now
she had died,
that blue-veined old woman had.

And now
each day had a beginning
and an end,
with a thousand hours in between.

Hours in which to open old albums
and miss his wife in glossy squares.

Hours in which to read old letters
and mourn his wife in black and white.

Hours in which to stand inside the closet,
for his wife's scent had not left with her,
but had clung,
foreign,
to that old woman and her clothes.

And now,
each day had a beginning and an end.

And a thousand hours in between
to cry at last,
the hot tears of a thousand days of loneliness
for his wife,
who had gone,
unexplained,
away,
and left behind only that blue-veined old woman
whose care would not let him mourn.

Autumnal Equinox

Entering the dark,
we look forward to a time of quiet,
of rest.

But here at the entrance,
there is still much light,
and warmth,
and sweet, red apples to be picked
for the gloaming quarter to come.

We approach the dark
surrounded by the energy of the passing sun quarter
concentrated into nourishing golden sheaves
and orange orbs.

Sleep will not start
until the lights are re-lit,
and we know,
once more,
the comfort of days
beginning their reach toward the sun.

America, 1993

"My brother-in-law sleeps in dumpsters."

He says it as I say,
   "My brother is a landscape contractor and
   my fiancé teaches English."

In San Francisco,
he relates,
of the upscale suburb
that his wife's brother Michael
finds suitable to his nighttime comfort,
they now pour Clorox in some of the dumpsters
to keep out vagrants.

Must be the same "they"
who say it will rain
and what colors are acceptable
this year
for bathroom towels and ski parkas.

He pulls on a tan jacket
and drives home through the snow.

His little clapboard house
folds into the forest-furred bottom ripple
of Purdue Mountain's flank.

As he opens the door
golden light flows out upon the porch boards

from the lamp beneath which his wife sits,
the blue-veined white melon of her breast
tipped by the pink
sucking
mouth of their child.

My lover and I drive through the falling, wet whiteness
walk up the silent lane,
sip brandy in bed,
sleep;
skins close as spoons in a flannel-lined silver chest
closed until the next Christmas dinner.

In San Francisco,
it is an hour past twilight.

Michael works the alley,
sniffing for telltale whiffs
of chlorine gas.

Weekend

I pull away,
and your freckles turn
to barbed wire
in my mouth.

I lean near,
and you are reflected,
reflected,
beside an arc
of glowing tungsten lamps;
repeated,
repeated,
across from me,
in the anti-matter
so near to where we sit.

Hesitate
and all will come,
as we will,
rolling on a mattress
of Vaseline and black olives.
The birds begin to sing,
and you rise,
to get out
your
gun.

Happy Birthday, Alex.
Your feet are cold,
as we walk through the puddles,
but champagne
and
olive pit spitting
make us steam
as you rub me
in the shower,
and I kiss the freckles
on your Irish shoulders.

We walk downtown
for pastries
and The Times,
for what is Sunday
without The Times?

We walk downtown
for pastries,
and I don't want anyone to see,
or say,
"Oh, she has the part, now."
The show has been so long on the road
that it's hard to say
who he'll have read for the part next,
or who
already has.

It is Sunday.
We were in bed until four o'clock,
and in Michigan
my mother takes codeine
for her headache.

In Virginia,
yours hopes that the neighbors have forgotten
that you avoided going into the army
by acting crazy.

I pull away,
and your freckles turn
to barbed wire in my mouth.

Happy Birthday, Alex.

Lingering Mirth

Empty wine bottles
raffia wrapped souvenir
of time spent with friends

Awakening From a Dream Of You

Your being
your thoughts
your presence,
filter through this room
like the remembered warmth
of spring sunshine
on the
winter-hunched
shoulders
of my soul

Cycles

The joyful amber scent of autumn,
of fruition complete,
begins to prevail
over the damp green redolence of summer.

Anti-Matter

Nothing matters.
Nothing really matters.
But I feel as if it matters that nothing matters.

I feel as if it all matters.

Such matters may be anti-matter.

There are whole villages constructed of anti-matter,
with fluted, green, cake frosting doorframes.
These villages stand in anti-matter places
corresponding to villages of matter,
where wood from forests is used for doorframes.

The inhabitants of the anti-matter villages
are creatures quickened from medieval woodcuts.

They move only in black and white,
and are descended
from a late-night orgy of griffins and gargoyles
above a cathedral in Salzburg,
where,
during the Gothic Period,
most people knew a lot about anti-matter
but didn't talk about it.

The inhabitants of the anti-matter villages
have had their lips removed at birth,
to give them permanent smiles
suggestive of rigor mortis.

Before holidays,
they creep softly, black and white out,
to stain their frosting doorways a deep red.

I cannot go to the anti-matter villages,
but from time to time
my lips are removed.

This frightens the inhabitants of matter villages,
so I must stay in the dark to remain myself.

Sometimes, though,
light forces its way through my wooden doorway,
and there are not places to hide.

Of course, after the people of matter
see my lips are gone,
they go, too.

The light goes first.

Before Solstice

Ten days till the sun returns.

Ten days till warm golden light
begins to quicken in the belly of time:
April's sap green buds,
May's lavender lilacs,
and the succulent, sweet, crimson strawberries
of summer solstice.

Now,
there are but ten more silent,
cold blue nights
until the sun returns.

The blood of my ancestors whispers its need.

Booted,
I plough through our whitened woods,
gathering greens:
pine, laurel, hemlock,
a few branches of red, rose hip berries.

Back in the house,
lamps lighted,
I stand them in vases,
lay them upon tables and shelves.

My blood knows,
answers,
fulfills,
the ancient lust for an act of trust
in greenness that will gestate
beneath a blanket of icy white days,
and silent, long, blue nights.

Basic Nature

Is there a basic nature?

In winning a struggle
with one's basic nature,
who wins?

What is lost?

Who loses it?

Breaking Trail

I break trail, lead the way, walk point,
stopping when we need one another,
to warm myself around the fires of our sisterhood;
to talk of that which you have seen,
but that I missed
upon the path,
and of the sun cycles ahead,
which I explore and map before you enter.

A truth I have found –
the trail markers of birthdays are not to be trusted.
They are messy things that don't line up in rows,
at even intervals,
like strung pearls.
More like apples, plumping and turning to ruby,
they fall into your hand
at some surprising moment,
when they recognize their own jeweled ripeness.

I felt myself turn thirty when I was yet twenty-nine,
and terminated, betimes,
that curdled decade of my twenties.

But despite the pile of surprise gifts
on the calendar-appointed date,
I didn't leave my thirties

till I'd spent a year or two
in the foyer of my middle decade,
licking the rich cream of my thirties
from my fingers
with flirtatious tongue flicks.

Thus began a true, ten year decade
that extended a while
past that golden celebration –
my attainment of a half century's collection
of mind maps,
and empty chocolate boxes filled with folded memories.

I have now lived,
my Little Sisters, as have you,
longer than most of those
ever to slip, wet and fragile,
into life upon the rounded breast of this misty blue ball.

And still,
I hunger for more.

As a dragon joyfully reveling in its jewels,
as a grandmother kneeling
with the smooth stones of her childhood rosary
slipping between fingers grown gnarled,
my heart in its ivory cage
beats me toward cronehood

with my hand cupped and uplifted.
In them: a precious stone for each birthday,
some dark, jagged, unpolished;
others glinting facets of iridescence.

They are strung into no neat necklace of attainment.
But oh, the texture
of that pile of pebbles mixed with gems!

And see!
There is room for more of these awards of each sun cycle
in my lifted, lusting palms.

Little Sisters,
cup your hands before you,
and follow me,
as I follow our mothers and grandmothers
into the decades.
It will be uneven going,
but precious stones will slowly mound
in the cup of acceptance
formed by your welcoming palms.

Curves

The banks of the steep mountain road
are softly mounded with pink laurel blossoms.
Their leathery green leaves glint
where the sun shines low and golden,
outlining a lacey coronet of veins
in the buffy rose ears
of a startled doe.

Gracefully,
my car slices around tight curves
in the lucid, amber light of early evening.

I move toward home
at the end of the day
when they called me at work
to say
I have
cancer.

Between the Dreamtime and the Day
In memory of Linda Buchanan

Between the stealthy sunrise
    Lightning pond, stone, loft, wood
    Your space – the place you made

And the abbreviated sunset
    Reflecting the day on crystal-strewn field
    Land you were bound to
    By more than you could name

There were words.

Balanced on the silence of too many wakeful nights
    On the edge of an empty ocean
    On the fine-honed edge of grief.

Between beginnings
    Promises kept and promises broken
    Each push of new life
    Sweetness of milk coming down

Between each long day
    Sacred morning barn silence
    High noon haying
    Meals prepared and eaten
    Graduations, weddings, birthings
    Hilarity and tears
    Each taking leave and each returning

Between your shy, graceful juke
        and the steel wall of your will

Between each long held endless breath
        That was your longing
        Each exhaled breath a reclamation

Between devastation and desire

There were words.

Between love remembered
        Love born anew
Between the dreamtime and the day

There were words,
There were words.

Voyage

Can I move backward
in time
to pick up
that which I was forced to leave;
that which I chose
to abandon?

Can I move backward
and find
love,
which was green
when I left it,
ripe, now,
and ready for me?

And what of
that which I have now?
Can I leave it?
Will it be here
in time,
when I return,
or must I carry it
with me,
into the past?

Change

Golden evening rays
   Slant warm through soft cricket song
     And dappled green

In the purple dark
  Growls thunder
    Wind rattles the summer from wet leaves

Silver morning air sits cool and still
  The scent of summer has blown away
    Autumn fills its place

Pre-dawn embers shift
and a small flame crackles high
for a bright moment

Christmas

The children climb
in and out
of aunts' warm, deep laps
up and down
the long legs of uncles and cousins,
whose laughter merges back in time
into that of their deep-sleeping fathers –
the uncles and cousins of my childhood.

We are Catholics, protestants, agnostics,
my husband and I the token
pagans in this room,
eating chocolate, cheese and wine –
cholesterol and diabetes be damned!

By this day,
and our suspended differences,
we are united in our love of these children,
and of the young people who rode scared, in a boat,
a century and more of Christmases ago,
to this new and wide place
where their children's children would grow
deep-lapped, and long-legged,
toward old age.

Abundance

I am like a pomegranate.
I am a pomegranate,
fulfilled and round with seeds –
of ideas,
of things accomplished and to be,
seeds of contentment,
a wealth of seeds –
enough to be wasted
to be spendthrifted
to be spent
in the richness of plenty.

Each seed,
each of millions,
encased in ruby wrappings – transparent,
jewel-red juice to flow crimson,
mouth-loved,
tangy sweet,
in chin dripping abundance
over my laughing face and naked body.
I am my seed.
I eat my seed.
I share.

Conjugation

My husband who teaches English
rants at his students,
  "Show us, don't tell us!
    Use action words!
    Get rid of the verb 'to be'!"

But today,
as the February sun practices for spring-bearing March to come,
I conjugate
that verb designed to validate existence.

"I am!"
sings my third eye, my dark, damp pineal gland,
absorbing sunshine through my forehead.

"You are!"
cry the husk-throated crows to one another,
I know, but with no false shyness,
I barge my way
into the feathered circle of their existence.
We've been neighbors for years, after all.

"He/she/it is."
These goats,
these cats, these squirrels,

these deer, these walnuts,
these shagbark hickories,
this wintergreen,
this partridge berry
require only the elegant syntax of a single verb.

"We/you/they are."
We are.
In the late winter woods,
the declaration is so simple.

We are.

Being Home

I sit in an environment
which I created,
and feel like God
on the seventh day –

"It is good."

Clowder Comfort

How comforting
to waken among cats
sleeping as soft as their fur.

Huff curls silkily,
grey and white,
beside the right pillow.

Jelly sits,
jade eyes round and alert in her silver face,
beside my left foot.

They hate each other,
but both love me,
and purr encouragingly as I slowly slip from somnolence.

Schwartz, as always,
has arisen before dawn,
from his special spot beside my face,
where,
in the night,
I can stroke him like a talisman;
coal-colored lover to my soul,
reader of my mind.

At the foot of the bed,
Susie cheerfully smoothes her calico coat,
though it is already pressed for the new day.

"Split, Baby."

She drew herself into a ball,
on her side,
with her knees under her chin
and her back to him.

"*Son of a bitch,*"
  he mumbled,
    deep in the thought of shoe lacing.

She had taken
hot white come,
and his cigarette,
and his self talk,
but after all that,
it was he
who could lick cunt
and not look at her face.

Esther

On a weathered palette
that I have pulled into the February sun,
Esther and I lean together.
Her tiny, shiny hooves folded beneath her,
she chews,
eyes closed,
trusting me with the vision of her safety;
a gift I guard well.

In the year since she emerged from a dying mother,
she has taught me much, this small leaf-eater.

Outsiders see it thus:
I have taken on an orphaned goat –
a lot of work for a pet.

But Esther and I,
inside a fragile, invisible, iridescent globe of love,
hum a silent harmony in which, as equals,
each gives what the other has not.

The goat-rooted word capricious means
"skittery, unpredictable."

As I sit beneath a Grandmother Pine
where the woods touch a small meadow,

Esther browses on pricker bushes,
clearing land for me,
eating overgrown blackberry canes with gusto,
thorns and all.

She allows herself to be lost for only a moment
in the bliss of each bite,
saving her languorous chewing for a safe place.

Here, she is prey,
her sweet, rounded silver haunches
that I groom carefully each day, with love and a brush,
a call to dine for dogs, coyotes,
maybe even the black bears that I never see
this close to the house;
all of them lean with winter hunger,
all of them with young
whimpering and yelping for flesh.

Esther knows she is flesh.
The spiral of DNA in each of her leaf-nourished cells
knows she is flesh.

Esther delights in her flesh,
She goat dances down the hill with me,
or around the kitchen,
which she still considers home,
after being raised in it.

She goat dances,
tossing her sweet, rounded silver haunches in mid-air,
to land half a compass turn
from where she ascended.

Esther delights in her flesh,
nipping and plucking at my pocket
for the dried apple bits she knows I have there;
fruit that will be sweet on the soft, pink flesh of her tongue.

Then, her wise, side-wary, innocent, golden goat eyes
scan the meadow.
Even with me beneath the Grandmother Pine,
she moves,
never staying in one spot for more than two bites.

She lowers her head to lift an oak leaf
that crackles satisfyingly as she chews.
She scans.
Then moves.

Esther knows she is flesh.
Her delight is her danger;
her capriciousness her safety.

I, hunted only by others of my kind,
and five times, by my own flesh,
need give up my predator's complacence
only in the cities of our making,

my disdain of capriciousness here in the woods
 a sort of noblesse oblige
that the small, the hoofed, the leaf-eaters can't afford.

Esther's rumen full,
we return to the weathered palette I have pulled
into the February sun.

Chickadees, bob, blue-grey,
through the winter air
between the spruce trees and their feeder.
High in the pines that ring our hollow,
crows make licorice chirring,
like ducks nurturing their young.

We lean together, on the silver boards,
and only Esther, my small teacher, and I
can see the opalescent pink rays of love

and learning

and trust

that flow between us
in the February sun.

Between New York and Nashville

For breakfast, I like bagels, with a lot of rich cream cheese,
and a record on the stereo – a Willie Nelson please.
Or, when it's time to party, and the others drink beer and toke,
just order me a Campari, while I snort a line of coke.

> *Oh, I'm halfway 'tween New York and Nashville*
> *and I just don't seem to know*
> *whether to study Bach and harpsichord,*
> *or rosin up the bow.*

My tastes incline to concerts – Waylon Jennings I'll happily hear,
followed by conversation
over tempura and Japanese beer.
Yes, the quiet of the countryside, it sets my soul at peace,
as I nibble on my feta cheese, and sip ouzo made in Greece.

> *Oh, I'm halfway 'tween New York and Nashville,*
> *and how hard it really seems*
> *to choose between Blue Ribbon*
> *and a Harvey's Bristol Cream.*

When I awake on Sunday to the village church's chimes,
I like to sip café au lait
and read the New York Times.
My neighbors in these mountains have an outhouse and a path,

but they don't mind and I sure don't,
as I read in my bubble bath.

> Oh, I'm halfway 'tween New York and Nashville,
> and if you are willing to play,
> I'd like to request a number
> by Hank Williams or Bizet.

Custom Made

I have always like riding in vans.
They have just the right
dashboard
slant
for putting
your feet
upon,
which makes them good places
for thinking,
for talking with someone,
and for feeling like yourself.

There

Dead,
The country of Dead.

Where is it?
A lot farther away than Altoona.

I'm afraid to look for it,
for once I find it, I must stay.

How could anyone
who brought me to shaking, livid rage
in which I flung my marriage ring back at him,
go to a place called Dead?

My mother and father went there, too.

I need them now,
but they left no phone number or forwarding address.

How could they leave me for a place called Dead?

How could anyone who awakened me with black coffee –
I prefer honey and cream,
but close *did* win the cigar that time –
to read to me from his autographed copy of W.B. Yeats,
Carlos Naiki on a flute made from an eagle's bone
laying in the soundtrack for those misty mornings in the woods,
go to a place called Dead?

The eagle went to a place called Dead, too.
Otherwise Naiki couldn't even have bribed that bone
out of him.

So many others have gone to that place.
Schwartz, Willie, Jelly, Lady Slipper,
Jasper, Corduroy, Mandrake,
Eddie May, Huff, Amber,
Tamerlaine, Nefertiti, Turtle, Alice,
Jimmy Cliff the Rastafurian…

I hope they hang with you, John –
that their furred greetings
are what caused your eyebrows to rise,
your lips form a perfect "O,"
with your last breath.

I thank you for sharing that last breath with me.

But I'm not going to search for you, John –
or any of the others,
for when I find Dead
I can never come back to these woods.

December

David's quasar,
   pentagram,
      sparkling bindi
         crescent moon,
            star of Bethlehem,

beacons all,
leads us through night's inky perturbation,
to scattered, tiny pockets in which trust and love
are kept aglow by the gentle breath of friendship,
to be carried out, when finally it is time,
to rekindle the warmth of
Peace on Earth.

Deep inside...

We are all sculptors,
> every blessed, rusted out F-150 driver of us;
> every busted Enron executive;
> every big haired, bar dancin' mamma of us;
> every young couple in a rented singlewide,
> foregoing pizza night to feed that puppy they found,
> and to save up for a down payment;
> every skinned out city woman fucking for a fix.

Deep inside,
> we all build precise and graceful sculpture,
> elegant enough to hang our selfness on for a lifetime,
> an architect's dream,
> carrying the story of that selfness longer than life.

Deep inside,
> we are all artists.

White-tailed Memories

I found a deer skull yesterday,
white and empty,
beneath a wild crabapple tree.
The jawbone and some teeth were tangled
in the brown scrub grass
beside it.

The skull was hollow,
and as white inside as out.
All the openings,
once filled with wet, living tissue
carrying messages
between the bright, moving outside,
and the dark, perceiving inside,
were vacant.
The eyes had dried,
or perhaps been carried away by crows,
leaving empty sockets.
The decaying of the spinal cord,
now part, perhaps, of the crabapples or the grass,
had opened the foramen magnum.

Opened?
Opened to what?
While the skull was filled with the wet, grey tracts
of electric charge

messages were neatly channeled
and contained within body and brain.
But when the dead and non-conductive cord
oozed into the ground,
what cloven-hoofed, ruminant perceptions
were allowed to diffuse
slowly
from the liquefying brain
through the now open orifices
into the quiet woods,
the silent universe?

What white-tailed memories
of tender-leafed, blue-skied summers,
of the power of autumn rutting,
of the rhododendron bark and growling bellies of winter
escaped into that crabapple orchard
to enter my thoughts
as things I have not learned,
but somehow know?

How much of my disquietude
as I walk back through the dark night,
between these silent mountains,
have I absorbed from the whispering air?
Fears loosed from the dead craniums
of those who came here alone,
before there were houses up the road a few miles,
before there were roads?

How much of the love which grows in me
with such power
such strength
that I can feel it quicken
as it gestates,
melted slowly from the quiet brains
of buried lovers
who knew,
each spring,
that their love was too strong to die with them,
and,
once dead,
sent it softly upward
into the air again,
in the veins of a lady slipper, or a trillium,
with its roots in the ground
over their white, once living skulls?

I found a deer skull yesterday,
white and empty.

Relative Stoicism

Someone shot the Pope today
and I have a cold.

A Polish man
who believes that there are rules to follow
in all situations.

A man who has a direct line to God
should he ever need it
though he probably won't push the
receive button for this incident
but keep on transmitting in
the hope of gaining
celibate glory
through
celibate stoicism.

A good man,
the Pope was shot today
and I have a sore throat
and a headache.

Lessons

Didn't anybody listen in high school?
In either Chemistry or American History?

Don't they remember that particles – all particles,
and all of us are particles within a greater system –
diffuse from an area of greater concentration
to an area of lesser concentration?

Not just those atoms and molecules safely contained
in Erlenmeyer flasks
upon the impervious slate countertops
of our long ago high school labs. No.
All particles, everywhere,
including those of the Karo syrup you just spilled,
spreading slowly across your kitchen floor

It means the particles of population called "people,"
following immutable laws, spreading
from areas of greater concentration of desperation –
Guatemala, Mexico, the Middle East –
into an area of lesser concentration of hunger and futility.

Didn't anybody pay attention when they were taught the
inescapable laws of nature?

And Lady Liberty –
surely they listened when we all were taught that she,

holding a light above our most open gate,
stands upon this base:
"Give my your tired, your poor,
your huddles masses yearning to breath free…"

Didn't they hear at least that in history class?

For Linda

A woman good.
A woman strong.
A woman gone.

This is the way of it.

She knew that.
Yet, along her way,
she eased the way
of those to follow;
her own people,
and others who needed easing.
And from her teaching,
they now know the ways of easing,
and extend the path of her immortality beyond sight.

This is the way of it.

Freeze Frame

It's easy to see:
their love is a calm, complacent habit.
She, a bird-like Gracie Allen of a woman.
He, tall, grey bearded,
considering, at sixty-five,
the start of a new career.
They, at ease
in the taken-for-granted
hammock of affection in which they rest.

After they leave the party,
she waits in the car
as he lopes up my front steps,
and into the kitchen,
to retrieve the dish they've left behind.

Suddenly,
he bends and kisses me on the mouth,
hard.

And that pressure
on my thirty-five year old lips says,
"Child,
you are tan, still,
your hair shines, still,
your skin is not slack, yet.
And my skin, my heat, my existence,

are slipping so fast away from me.

Let me use this kiss as a nail
on which to hang a single moment,
to halt for a second,
the sliding of my flesh into eternity."

His fingers brush only my shoulder,
then he walks back down my porch steps,
sticky Pyrex pan in hand.

"Good night," I call,
across decades of tanned skin,
and varicose blue veins, and a single instant
of stopped time.

Arid Spaces

To know
the juices of one another's bodies
is good,
even
necessary;
But it is not enough.

Vows

I want us to grow old in each other's arms.

If I must trade in the
    pink nipples
    and tan skin of youth,

I want to trade them for
    walks in the weeds beside you,
    parties where I feed people and you sing to them,
    quiet evenings of just being together,
    whole days spent loving and cuddling
    and ignoring the phone together.

If I must give up
    my flashing,
    golden-copper tan,

I want to give it up for
    a rioting grey cloud
    surrounding a face made calm
    and strong
    by years of touches from your eyes.

If I must see your tall and cheerful body
    begin to limp
    or steep
    or stiffen,

I want it to be in a nest we have made together,
>   where we can eat the fruit of trees we have planted,
>   then sleep,
>   skins touching.

Skins that will be as warm as children's,
>   on bodies polished
>   with the craftsmanship
>   of two whole lives
>   of loving.

Peeling Beets

A moiré of purple reds.
The smell of earth
turned into living cells
of tuberous red fiber.
The knife slices into my thumb,
and the blood mingles with
beet juice.

Keepers

For women, it's the dishes and jewelry.

> "This brooch was my Aunt Ellen's.
> I don't think it was expensive,
> but I remember her wearing it to church every Sunday.
> It's mine, now."

The brooch rests,
now rarely worn,
inside a jewelry box.
A gold filigree connection
to childhood.

The bread pans were my grandmother's.
Now they sit on a shelf beside a tin of SpaghettiOs,
making a house with ranch trim seem
as if the kitchen were real.

The tools speak to men.

When my Uncle Charlie died, Anna (that's my aunt) said,

> "I don't know what to do with the stuff in the garage.
> I don't even know what most of it is.
> You take what you want, Honey.
> Charlie'd want you to have it."

Grandpa's sickle hangs on the wall in a suburban garage.

"This here was Charlie's drill press.
A fine machine.
Nope, I ain't used it yet,
but it was too good to go to strangers."

"…and that ballpeen hammer,
the one with the head all rounded off
so's you can't hit anything straight on with it,
that's the one my dad used
when we built the new garage
the summer I was sixteen."

That spark-striking steel
once connected board to batten,
but fastens now,
the past
to the future.

1970

was the year I fell in love with the Goodyear Blimp,
and though I haven't seen it for years,
a funny feeling still comes when I think about it.

The celebration of some special occasion
caused it to spend about a week
hovering,
good-naturedly ostentatious,
contentedly,
silvery phallic,
above our town.

At night
it gave me flirtatious, winking light shows
to the background drone of its engines.

They were, of course,
not for me.
They were just the Blimp's way of being.
But I preferred not to think
about all the others feeling the light shows,
and caressing the Blimp's erotic bulge
with their eyes.

A few people –
I don't know how they were chosen –

got to ride in the little basket beneath its belly.
Like a fourteen year old,
I worshipped it without going near.

After a few days it left.

Lana's Kitchen

Lana and I
peel and stir,
knead and bake.

Lana's mother,
Stella,
wrapped in the soft blanket of age,
sits in a rectangle of sunshine
thrown by the window.

In her silent thoughts,
I can see
lovely ladies
wearing flowered silk dresses.

For Shadow

Once joyful,
hard-muscled,
sheathed in chocolate brown velvet,
these bones danced an ivory pas de deux
with butterflies;
predator and prey
glinting in the golden sun.

Now, too long,
has this bony old frame ached.
Creaking silently,
she creeps through long, green grass,
finds a soft, sun- warmed hollow
and sleeps.

Catcher at last
a blue-jeweled butterfly,
brown as rain-fresh earth,
feels the spirit breathed softly upward
from sun-warm fur,
and carries it lightly
upon the powdered velvet of her wings,
circling higher,
higher,
in the golden light.

In a White Coat

I hang posters in my office,
to tell people who I am.

They say I can't take time,
the Blues, and the administrator do,
to explain to people that they can trust me
with their bellies full of pain-fire,
their three month old babies,
the cancer eating jagged bites
from their faiths and their futures.

I hang posters in my office.
"Here," say the pictures,
"are the things I believe in.
Here's what's important to me.
Let them allow you to know me enough
that you walk in scared,
yet can talk to me
about the way your guts are destroying your dreams."

Georgi Johnson

Your mother's travail
spared mine
the labor to birth you.

And yet,
when you walked into that mountain cabin,
on a crystalline, snowy night,
our blood recognized itself,
and our lives entwined as sisters.

Our names,
for four decades have separated us
by but a single letter,
but in the Old Country,
our great grandmothers shared a name,
and knew their kinship,
as we did not,
till four winters passed.

And now,
four winters it's been,
and springs, and summers and Samhains,
that we have laughed together,
no words needed
to tell the other why,
that we have picnicked in quiet
on red wine and cheese.

Golden-haired Amy,
mirror-image of your graduation picture,
has softly settled into an open niece niche,
padded with the affection of shared blood
reaching back across generations
to the snowy land of our Grandmothers
born under the midnight sun.

And now,
another gift you offer
the joy of cooking your wedding feast,
of bearing witness
as you accept this good man to husband you,
in the warm brown house beneath winter stars,
and so,
bring into my life
a brother.

Going Home

How strange –
the album of my memory
shows modern costumes on its snapshots.
I can't turn back and page through
the remembered times
and people
and places preserved on mental Kodak paper
between the convoluted brain pages.

No…
each scene,
each picture,
in mockery
of recorded history,
has been retouched to what it was not,
in the realness of my childhood.

And,
I turn a page to find
the lacquered image of the field paths
where I played, but see instead,
bramble-thick woods, without indentation.
Page after page mocks the clarity of my memory.

Girls and mothers have white hair
and fat stomachs,

where brown curls and innocent bodies
had been pasted in with triangular corners.

I try to remember, and believe,
that I was the photographer,
not the photographed,
and that I have only come back
to look for some film.

Reaching

Inside my hands
are the hands of a singing child
with hair not yet darkened to brown.
Her unshapen face
smiles up at green leaves
made translucent by sunshine.

Inside my outstretched,
thirty-three year old body,
which will someday be sixty-three,
the child still stretches up
toward the summer of life.

Home

I have emptied out the closets, almost.
In one, I've left an old corduroy shirt of my father's,
to put on when I work
then return to the hook.

Two of my mother's watches
remain in her top dresser drawer;
already, mouse droppings litter the empty ones.

From out of them
I have sorted nylons with runs –
she never switched to panty hose –
and flat packs of unopened pairs;
old white underpants with stretched elastic,
never thrown away
till I stuffed them into bags I labeled "Goodwill,
mixed with the ones that were still good;
a metal box filled with letters
written by my brother's friends, and mine, to my parents
after we had all left,
for college, for Viet Nam, for nursing school.
I sort the letters into piles,
one for me, another for my brother,
pour coffee, carry my pile to my mother's chair and read.
I keep the emptying house alive –
beds made;
long-replaced pictures of ancestors,

and of us, in tykehood,
restored to prominence on living room shelves;
flowers from the yard in a vase on the table.
I plant red geraniums in the planter
where they have always grown,
though I shall leave in another week.

I walk to the edge of the woods
where a tree stump – humus now –
once housed the fairies
who left tiny gifts on our bedside tables.
Those homeless fairies still watch over the graves
of cats, puppies, found rabbits and birds,
watered with our tears into the sandy soil
between the scrub-wild
and our rangy-tame yard.

When I return in the spring,
my brother and I will empty
the outbuildings and the garage –
never in my half century occupied by a car,
so full it is of the father-smelling tools
and ropes and machines.

And after that,
after that,
where shall I go,
when I need to go home?

Buoyancy

We bob,
   complacent,
grasping the safe edges of the dock

But the tides rip us loose, betimes
   struggling and weeping,
into the current

When finally we stop resisting,
   we rise, able to breathe and float,
supported by the flow

Some we see around us fight,
   fight against the current,
fight to return to the secure mirage of harbors,
receding in the distance

But we float, able to breathe
   supported by the flow
and reach out our hands to one another

Cinereal Tides

It was the end of the cycle
again.
She knew it so well, it was always the same.
The fight to keep from slipping
back down the slide,
and always ending up at the bottom anyway,
and never believing
that there would be another crest.

Although, when she rode the ridges
she always knew that being on the top, in the air,
was only the beginning of the trip,
the slip, the slide,
back to the bottom, and beneath,
where there was only grey numbness.

That's what bothered her most.
After all, black depression was at least passionate,
and understandable,
but the greyness…

Well, she supposed that's where the end would be.
In greyness – how ignominious.
It was bearable.
That's what made it so frightening –
It was just barely bearable.

Sentience

I know how it is.
Ya just don't get around to stuff.
It must be going on three years
that I first noticed those little feeder calves –
one black steer, one brown –
in the small pasture behind a house down our road.

Both of 'em part Hereford, must be, by their white faces,
destined for somebody's freezer by November.

But they grew, then wintered over;
repeated the cycle, drinking from the summer-warmed run,
Near companions lying down for afternoon ruminations,
sheltering from sleet
in their jury-rigged lean-to.

It was last Thursday that I didn't see the black one
from my Subaru's passing window.
Nor again the next day,
or since.

That Big Black Guy,
that hunk of beef on legs,
was raised for this:
neatly shot between the eyes,
flayed, sawn,

wrapped in white paper,
he lies now in parcels,
between discount pizzas
and an unfinished half quart of Cherry Garcia.

His tawny companion of all those many rosy dawns,
heated noons, livid sunsets,
drinks water still
from Moose Run,
and lies down quiet, to chew his regurgitated hay.

Did they butcher the Black Guy in front of him,
I wonder,
right in the pasture?
Does the Brown Guy's placid face belie a horror
that he could not speak,
if he could speak?

Oh, I do go on!

You know what they say,
"They don't feel pain the same way as us white folks."

What?

Your expression —
Did I say something wrong?

Rebel Yell

It's because I love you,
my mother and my father,
that I fight,
that I am a rebel,
that you think I am weird.
I fight for you.

I live a life of "different than" because you deserved
so much you didn't get,
my mother and my father.

You worked so hard
and were damaged so,
crippled so
by the very ways you fight to defend from change.

And I fight too,
I learned that from you,
so that, though I fear it may never come,
there may be a time, sometime,
when some,
who are as beautiful as you used to be,
are not so afraid of life
that they struggle to cling to
the unchanging state
which is their cage.

It Works

My very first herb teacher said it would.
I've read since, that it's traditional
       to use ground ivy for headaches –
the sinusy, snuffy kind.
I've taught it too,
along with chamomile tea
       for bloating,
cayenne for arthritis,
black cohosh during menopause
right there
in the exam room,
in my white coat, speculum dangling from one hand.

But what would those patients think,
the ones who pay at the front desk,
to see the healer in white coat,
to see me,
limp upon my bedspread,
bedraggled cloth upon my eyelids
crunched up,
green,
pungent
ground ivy leaves
sticking out of my nostrils?

Programming Error

I wish I could be
as seductively rational,
as cybernetically logical,
as the brain
of the IBM iron maiden
which you so passionately court and mindfuck each day.

I wish my circuits had been neatly printed
with molten metal
upon a board –
a module to be replaced when it inconveniently shorts out.
But instead, my synapses
require the untidy dampness
of an interstitial fluid composed of
sweat, and cunt juice;
sperm and blood;
hormones and coffee with cream;
and a minimum daily requirement of love,
along with other depressingly unreliable organic ingredients.

It's probably okay, though.
The salinity of my periodic,
unprogrammable lacrimations
would undoubtedly have rusted
the RJE terminal of your life.

Foiled

I've tried to build an ivory tower
for myself.
In fact,
I've even succeeded in the construction,
but I can't seem to inhabit it.
It's like putting a fat lady in a girdle,
where she kind of overhangs,
and bulges out the top and bottom.
And I find
that my ivory tower girdle
leaves
red indented
elastic marks
on the waistline of my wishes,
and garter imprints
on the wishing-to-spread
thighs
of my existence.

Jimmy the Woodsman

My friend, Jimmy the woodsman,
says that animals all go down to the creek to die.
He pronounces it "crick",
which sounds better somehow
in the hushed woods.

The dogs,
the deer,
the chipmunks and squirrels
leave their bodies beside the water
to bloat,
then flatten,
to turn as grey as mud,
then finally when only white bones are left,
to be randomly,
impersonally,
lovingly,
washed away
one by one
in the sweet,
clear,
rushing
floods of spring.

For Three

Glossy hair,
glinting in the sun.
Hard, strong young muscles,
levering pearl-covered bones
mother nourished into perfection,
bunch for
leaping.

Hard metal,
with sound too loud to perceive,
to understand,
punches through
the perfect young one.

Fractured splinters
and shredded meat
lie on cold earth,
encased in grit caked hair.
Metal does not know.

Flair

Wrought
by a half century's pounding and polishing,
my well-formed coppery aegis
strikes upon yours –
intricate as mine,
shining silver,
and even longer in the crafting.

Stars
sparkled in the clashes
shine
brightly as those spinning behind my eyelids
every time we make love.

Each impact of intrusion
striking upon deep-grained habit,
is the gem-cutter's blade
releasing diamond glints
as perfect and permanent
as Venus glowing above the sunset.

Unconventional Scholar

I am majoring in wisdom,
but the curriculum
is available
only in the form
of independent study.

My thesis
shall be scribed
in snow angels,
to the heads of which
a few grey hairs adhere,
shed from my scalp
as I lie spread-eagled, to print them
in clean,
wise
rows upon the ground.

Grateful Mentor

Little one,
the tiny curls against
your fragile,
thin,
beautiful
five-year old nape
make me want to cry.

How perfect you are,
how vulnerable,
as you lean,
intent,
sorting pebbles from the hole you just dug.

You do me honor
simply by sharing existence
and by offering – though you don't yet know you do so –
anticipation of the time
when I'll show you
how to spit watermelon seeds over the porch rail;
and give you the illicit glee
of eating cookies in the woods
for breakfast,
and staying up past bedtime
when you are old enough to visit
without your mother.

How I wonder about the ways
that my musings about my own earthy beliefs
will season
the robe-cloaked codes
you are now beginning to lisp.

I feel so much a child myself
as I run with you on the beach,
hold your hands tightly
as we squeal into the waves.

Not yet so venerable as a grandmother,
nor so burdened with responsibility as a mom,
I glory in the gift you give me –
aunthood.

Sacred Ceremony

I found her when the snow melted,
late February, it must have been.
The ivory xylophone among wet leaves was her spine.
You'd think I'd have noticed sooner,
she was so close to the trail.

I stood, studying her bones,
lying like a puzzle in the damp duff,
some still bound together by tenacious tendons.
Others were clean, though,
and in one hand, I carried down to the house,
the ivory palace of her skull,
and an alabaster femur.

Against the dark, rough boards of our porch wall,
I hung that cervid cranium.
Below it, in a basket on the floor,
I gently placed the leg bone so perfectly synthesized
of mother's milk, acorns, pine needles.

Now, each time I walk up the trail,
I return with more of her
to fill that basket on our back porch.
Her spine is still as intact as when it laced together
a graceful leap across the bracken
and damp moss beside a spring.

I handle the bones gently,
awed at their intricacy,
aware of the intense intimacy of my act.
I have found no broken ribs,
no violation of her creamy skull.

Slowly, as the animals clean them,
I carry more of that exquisite, osseous sculpture
into the shelter of our porch,
to rest respected.

And with each blanched bone I pick up,
then put to rest in a basket
that once held a half bushel of ripe, redolent peaches,
I silently question,

"How is it that I am so certain of the necessity for this?"

Trev

My feet were always warm when I was a child
Or, could I have slipped on a fog-damp flagstone of memory?
Surely I must,
once,
have had cold feet
before I freed myself of my parents' nest in the woods.

Thirty,
my father was, when I was born.
Babies?
He knew nothing of them.
My grandmother,
giggly Grandma Co,
my mother's mother, the Mayor's wife,
provided a piece to the puzzle when she told my father,
"You can tell if a baby is cold by feeling its feet."

So each night he arose
four times, maybe five,
and stepped silently to my crib –
in youth, he had taught himself
to walk in the woods more quietly than a deer –
turned back the covers and felt my feet,
the one thing he knew for certain how to do for a baby.

This baby of his,
this baby girl he had made with the Mayor's beautiful daughter,
would never have cold feet.

I can still now feel,
half a century later,
that silent nighttime vow
made in the memory of cardboard-lined shoes.
He told us about those.

About how,
after leaving the mother whose broom
whistled through the air at his head,
the father who slept in the basement smelling of bathtub booze,
he spent his teen years roaming through the Depression.

Inside his shoes was cardboard,
to fill holes worn hitching down pot-holed blacktop
toward places where he heard there might be a job.

He told us of the kerosene lantern –
swaying firebomb, the only source of heat –
propped beside his numb legs
in the freezing cab of the tractor trailer he drove,
till that trucking company went bankrupt with the rest.

Told of the tire iron beside him as he geared down into
tight curves where highwaymen lurked,
desperate for anything to sell in that time of Great Want.

He told us, too, how he learned to play harmonica
shirt stuffed with folded newspaper to keep out the sleet-filled
wind,
in hobo jungles,
when there were no jobs.

It must have been in one of those jungles,
packing board shanty walls
keeping out most of the snow,
with young men sleeping close together in all of their clothes,
that some half-grown boy,
contributing his body heat to the rest
coughed living death, unseen, into the midnight air.

Trev didn't know it.
No one did.
For nearly sixty years,
his strong body
kept those microscopic shreds
of a sick boy's puff of steam
sealed in a tiny pod within his lungs.

Then,
the cold dark web eating his breath
more silently than my father could stalk a deer,
tore open that pod
and let January blow out of his chest;
the cold of those jungles,
the cold of a boy alone,
with his only home the memory of a father sloshing in at dusk
and a mother screaming.

That boy,
that shivering boy,
afraid so often during cold numb years
of newspaper and cardboard,
grew up to marry the Mayor's beautiful daughter.

And never,
ever,
were their children's feet cold.
And never,
ever,
did he say to me, "I love you."

But even when,
fully grown,
I went back to sleep in the bed of my childhood,
I'd awaken in the mornings
to find my bathrobe laid across my feet.

And never,
ever,
did he shiver alone, inside again,
for nearly sixty years,
till TB and cancer
drained all his breath
through that hale of winter
inside his chest.

Mary of the Moon

Child blossom,
born beneath silver light,
perfect in the now of our arms,
yet
you promise the fruit of the future.

Mary of the Moon,
Equinox child,
daughter of the perfect balance between night and day,
between summer and autumn,
your birth gives us proof,
yet again,
that Goddess and God,
Sun and Moon,
Summer and Autumn,
all are faces
of the One
whose true and speakable name is Love.

Mary of the Moon,
on this day
we present to you your brothers and sisters,
children, too,
of that power:
Autumn and Summer,
God and Goddess,
Sun and Moon.

With them
work and dance,
bring forth the fruits of your labor and laughter,
and know
that their true and speakable name,
and yours,
is neither
Yahweh nor Astarte.
Not Allah,
not Jesus,
not Mary,
or Innana,

but Love.

Morning Redolence

Through silver-soft light,
imaginary foxes
pace beneath our window,
sniffing, sniffing.

Slowly,
I sense them,
drawn by the scent of our love
trapped musky, between my skin and the sheets.

The separating edges of my sleep
are tinted the shade of a contented rose,
by the sweet fox lure of last night's lust.

Then,
from the coffee you bring,
brown velvet vapors
send back those vulpine visitors,
unfulfilled,
to seek their own heat
within night shadows,
still shading
deep and ferny places.

Seconds

I am thirty-three now,
and,
when I am still
I can hear the soft rustling
of the minutes moving past.

The seconds
sometimes brush softly against my face
when I am quiet and alone,
or when,
with you,
I pick the perfect, waxy blossoms
of friendship;
or when,
with you,
I look at the partly unfolded petals
of love.

John

"How is John?" you ask.
How is John? How is my husband?
I'll tell you how my husband is.

He's always been a brilliant, charming wordsmith
with an incendiary temper,
who wears tight, black leather jeans,
and palindromes for earrings.

And still he is a brilliant, charming wordsmith
with holes eaten in his brain
by a disease called dementia, that just keeps eating, eating.

Last week, I told the doctors to begin phasing out the medicine
which slows the boring of holes in his brain.
For him, I spoke the words that he would speak,
were there no holes in almost all the word nests of his brain.

The medicine does not plug the holes.
It is not a plug.
Not *the* plug.
But I pulled it.
"Let's get this over with,"
My husband would say, if he had words.
That's how John is.

November

This cold, pellucid light
has come again,
filtered, it seems,
through a nacreous lens.

The landscape lies illuminated
as a heathered rainbow.

Soft, soft, the wistful spectrum of November,
spelling October's menopausal bloom.
Her labor passed,
Her flowering and fruition complete,
the Earth lies at rest in crepuscular shades.

Ocher stubble stretches toward the flanks
of gently rolling mountains;
purple, mauve, rhododendron and pine green,
iridescent as an opal at twilight,
velvety as a grandmother's quilt,
ridges black furred with unleafed trees
against a sterling silver horizon.

Chilled now, despite my wool and denim,
I crunch through ashen ruby leaves
toward our small, brown house.

Spittin' in the Wind

I love those
juicy,
slimy,
sticky
four-letter,
Anglo-Saxon expletives.
To use them
is to spit into the wind,
from a dandy upwind position.

Unlike
tiny, crystalline drops
of inadvertent, conversational saliva spray,
dissipating, forgiven, into the air,
those throat-felt Scandinavian syllables
Thwacks! satisfyingly
against reality,
then slide slowly downward,
in silence,
leaving phlegmy snail trails
upon its carefully polished façade.

Snapshots

Some paper images you pass,
of other women I surmise,
as I lean silent
upon the pillows of your bed,
and know
that the omissions
spare the pain of memory for you,
that of measurement for me.

You close the wooden box.
We sleep.

Upon awakening,
we bathe the dog,
then one another,
in the clearing outside your house.
Warm water
makes diamond rainbows in golden morning sun.
I soap your shining silver mane
and hold
the dark haired young man
who strode long leggedly
through the realness of wars,
the realness of passing years,
and women,
into my arms.

Demeter Waiting

No arbutus yet,
flowers beneath crackling oak leaves
on this early
April afternoon.
But in the woods,
a floral scent
drifts upon the gusting breeze.
Pussy willows,
I am sure,
for already their catkins have burst into
pollen-dusty drapes,
buzzed about by winter hungered bees.

And then,
to the left of the trail –
a tree
diaphanously cloaked in parchment-colored veil.
My breath sucks itself
I stand motionless with a pleasure
now a year forgotten,
and plunge into brambles
just to get near
this early-blooming
cherry.

But no, as I approach,
I see a dogwood,

draped still,
in last year's leaves,
brittle, curled,
translucent and pale
as the blossoms my eyes expected.

I stand.
The sun sparkles from those leaves,
polished as no nearby bud,
by a year of soft rain,
pounding storms,
grating sleet.
Each leaf drapes
the end of an elegant curve of twig.
Each leaf waits
for the bud beneath
to push it form its year-old place.
Early silent leaf waits
as perfect and pale
as the petals that soon will replace it
in exhausted celebration
of a new spring.

I venerate

and walk up the mountain
to sit beneath low pines
in the sleeping places of deer.

Beholden

Come and hear the fog-wrapped morning.

The sound of grey and black geese,
unseen above the formless sky,
pulling spring northward behind them.

The flapping, raucous ruckus of crows
decrying our invasion
of their damp, stubble fields.

The distant, subliminal drone of diesels
draying the plastic-wrapped dreams
through the periphery of our awareness.

The drop of tiny, glass-clear, beads of water
from feathery, five-tufts of white pine needles
onto the slippery, brown duff beneath.

Our soft footfalls on sodden leaves
becoming silence
as we stop to listen.

Cicada Summer
For Bib, pregnant only a month

Leaving sienna and silver-winged bodies behind,
they creep
once more,
into an earthy bed.

The hot air grows still.

When again we hear
cicadas' raucous celebration
of freedom,
honeysuckle breezes
and mating lust,
I shall be an old woman,
silver and wise in our sienna-roofed house;
you will be ready
for your croning celebration;
and the tiny, warm, pink dot of love within you
will have begun to sing
its own hormone-strung melodies.

Upon Learning a Friend's Husband Has Cancer

My husband carries death in his head.
We walk to the mailbox,
on this day after he comes home to me,
only as far as the mailbox together,
and he must take a nap when we get home.

A nap,
my man takes a nap,
after just a walk to the mailbox.
This man who walks a fifteen minute mile every day,
sometimes twice,
must lie down
after we take the death in his head
for a walk,
only as far as the mailbox.

Just two weeks it's been
since last he did a fifteen minute mile,
early autumn sunshine dappling his path down the lane;
only a week and a half
since he started the medicine for bronchitis,
medicine that didn't work,
because there is death in my husband's chest.

Silently,
he carries death.

What day did it begin?
The day we planted carrots together, last spring,
crumbling the earth,
grown black with the years of our loving it?
The day the kids came home,
with all their babies and dogs,
for the reunion?
He looks so good in the picture of that day,
the grey in his hair distinguished,
the curls of his beard jaunty.
How often I have twined my fingers in that beard
as we lie together,
bellies round with middle age,
but skins as warm as the youth we never shared.
When did death begin to grow in this man
that I didn't find
till all of our kids were nearly grown?

Silent,
so silent,
he carried it first beneath the skin of his strong back,
in his kidney.
The doctors found it there, silent still.
Aren't kidneys to make your body clean?
How can they poison my man?
How can they send death,
silent, so silent,
into his mind,
into his breath?

His breath is so short, now,
the warm breath that blows against the back of my neck
as we sleep
with our old skins touching.
How much is left to blow soft
against my sleeping skin?
Warm skin,
warm breath,
cooling, cooling.

My husband carries death in his head.
And as it grows,
the hot blood drains
through holes
that silent screams are tearing in my heart.

Juxtaposition

My own first name
is my mother's middle,
hidden,
one.

A cosseted name!
A signature protected and flanked –
as the pregnant mother's flanks
enclose her unborn child in safety –
by the politely smiling first and last names.

And in that safe, protected, flanked
middle of the written face of me,
nestles
the first name so windblown,
exposed and battered,
during the three quarters of a century
that my father wore it.

Coronation

Now
is the time
when I can withhold my life's blood
for my own need.

Now
I no longer must monthly scour
the dark, warm, sacred space of my womb room
to make it ready for a guest of nine moon cycles
who may not come.

Now
I replace the childhood gold –
beautiful with the monochrome of youth –
and grow in its place a silver crown,
radiating rainbows in the sun.

Now
I have earned my face,
my body.
No longer unformed,
they are the clear journal of my life:
each line, shadow and softening
a tracery telling tales
of all I have so far been.

Yet,
as when I was a maiden curved and smooth,
still now,
secrets lie deep within my unseen dark,
nourished by the warm blood
that I must no longer give away.

Artisan Strife

I struggle to think in metal.
The molecules of my brain,
soft, grey,
flowing with warm, saline juices,
strive to slow, to ionize,
to bond my thoughts to one another
as tightly as the ionic,
rose-pink grasp of copper –
daughter,
as am I,
of our Mother, the Earth.

My saw works slowly
through the flesh of my mother's metallic child,
releasing an image of our sisterhood.

Stumble

I'm back on my stride again!

Oh no –
I've fallen off track,
limping,
showing my wounds,
feeling them,

But it's there.
I had it for a minute, so I know I can get it back –
that mental boot walk,
that stride that gives me an invisible cowgirl hat.

Never fear, I'll get back
to my old heel-clunking, hip-swinging mosey,
the one that says,
 "Don't mess with this mama,
  she's likely to ignore you right into oblivion."

But first,
I have to pull these mental cowgirl boots up over some scars,
and I may have to lean a little,
sometimes,
when I get tired.

Postlogue by my friend Lana, who read this hot off the yellow legal pad

"It's a good poem,
I'm glad you're writing.

Please know you can lean on me.
And if I'm tired too, we can both lean on a lamp post
until we're ready to walk on."

Peach breath
steams
the crinkly, transparent bag
I carry home from the farmer's market.

A downy, curved caress upon my lips…
And then I bite!

O juice!
O Peach!
It's summer!

Beneath

Beneath a rippling, crystalline cloak,
the Earth slumbers,
gestating,
even in her dreams,
the birth of Spring.
Nourishing its fragility
in that thin,
tender space
where breathy white drifts
spread sharp, icy fingers
into loamy, chocolaty soil.

Like baby bears,
translucent and pink,
suckling
upon their curved and sleeping mother,
beneath brown ground,
I curl myself against your back
beneath a down coverlet,
as silent snowfall mounds, diamond white,
around our small brown house.

The Letter

My former husband,
a good man,
writes
to tell me
of his parents' move
to an assisted living apartment.
They will be close to his sister.

And three hundred miles
from the town,
from the tan house,
into which they carried
their first
prayed for,
black-haired, red-faced baby –
and later, three more –
home from the hospital,
nearly sixty years ago.

His carefully placed longhand
looks like
a dry and silent tear upon the page.

My Honky-Tonk, Rickey-Tickey, Country-Western, Hillbilly, Tear-Jerking, Beer-Sloshing Song For David

Well, I knew when I first met ya
that I never would forget ya,
you were the answer to my dreams.
But remember that I warned ya
so that I would never harm ya
that I was competent in each of just three scenes.

> **Chorus:**
>
> *Oh I can cook and write and screw,*
> *and I've done them all for you;*
> *I screwed you up*
> *I cooked your goose,*
> *then wrote this song for you.*

For two years I've kept you fed,
and I've also warmed your bed,
but Baby these are only two
of three things that I need,
now I'm askin' to be freed
to be by myself and think what I must do.

> **(Chorus)**

It's not easy, now, to go,
for David, well I know,
you've taught me more than I had ever known.
Oh we'll share some time again,
and we'll be much more than friends,
but for now, the times we've had are just outgrown.

   (Chorus)

Mirage

Your Being,
Your Thoughts,
Your Presence,
Filter through this room
like the remembered warmth
of spring sunshine
on the
winter-hunched
shoulders
of my soul.

Terminal Tutoring

I am practicing to die –
to conquer my fear of death
as I am conquering,
slowly,
my fear of water
by swimming – by learning to control myself in it.

To glide beneath the surface,
not as skillfully,
it is true,
as one who is taught from childhood
to conquer fear
by taking control
of one's own destiny,
but with increasing strength.

The symbols,
the flowers –
used to distract one's attention
from the reality of
death make one weak – cause one to have to face
the eventual
alone reality
without practice,
struggling, and screaming,
and trying to hold back,
from what will surely be.

I do not seek death – my life is too rich,
too good,
too textured, to wish for its end.

But even kings
die of things
which make them
puke
and spit
and smell bad.

My mother believes
that if you do not put flowers
on the graves of your relatives –
the right kind of flowers,
and at the right intervals –
you did not love them.

Now You See
(Salesman's Instructions)

"Now you see,
this hose attaches here –
and please notice
the *Never Fail Hose Lock*.

I'm sure you've had it happen
when you're sweeping –
you give a tug and whoops –
the hose comes loose from the tank.
Now, with our *Never Fail Hose Lock*
that can't happen.
No Sir, oops, I mean Ma'am –
My goodness, anyone can see
you're not a sir –
The only way you can get the hose
off this vacuum cleaner
is to push this little button.
Yep, right here, pulls off easy,
but not until you want it to.

Another unique feature
of our machine,
two really,
are the retractable cord
and the catering service.

I mention them together
because they're powered by the same mechanism.
Now the cord retracts when you step on this switch,
course you've got to be sure
to unplug it first,
otherwise
you're likely to be pulling down
electric poles for 3 or 4 miles.
That's how good the mechanism is,
and just this year
we've come out with a new feature –
just turn this dial to "C"
step on that switch
and you activate the catering service.

Yes Ma'am,
due to the wonders of science –
and our own Research and Development Department –
always working to make your life a little easier –
we can now offer you,
for only three extra dollars a month,
a catering service
capable of preparing
any one of three hundred and forty
different menus
suitable for anything
from family reunions
to wedding receptions.
Now you know how you
wear yourself to a frazzle

whenever you have 20 or 30 folks
for dinner.
Well, now you can enjoy
your own get-togethers.
Yes Ma'am,
just set this dial on "C"
step on the switch
and go get dressed.

Our machine
takes all the work out of entertaining.
The index of menus
is in the operating manual
and the menu selector
is right down here."

Morning

Three eggs
sit in a shallow, white porcelain bowl,
on the yellow
table top.

Grand Research

Perhaps
God listens,
with head cocked to one side,
like a meditative terrier,
in his unperceived-by-humans form,
as we squirm,
and scream,
and importune,
and screw,
and make patterns in the landscape,
and die.
While he takes
kindly,
puzzled,
scientific
notes.

My lover
has discovered another woman.
It turns out
that I am not the official
U.S. Bureau of Standards
instrument for measuring reality.

Woman

Strong of limb,
tan of unmarked skin,
tangled tresses trailing in the air
as you stretch upward to leap and dance,
or tousled
as you recline in lust, then labor,
look with love and awe upon your pudendal flower.
Purple-pink, succulent with life's blood,
diademed with a pink pearl of pleasure,
its flamboyant petals are rooted upward
into a velvet-lined, scarlet ovoid,
the strong, soft, sizeless site of motherhood.

So quickly grew those ruffles of delight
from the peach-hued promise of its natal day.
No flower, then, or life's blood was there,
but only a creased, pink bud
hid
between untried, folded, perfect limbs.
Down, so like a peach,
misted over your smooth scalp then;
and lines of blue, thread thin,
showed beneath the lucid skin
of your infant belly
guarding
the tiny, pink almond which would,
one day grow strong enough

to bind your womanhood
to your motherhood.
So brief, too, will be the time
till your beauty is crowned
in thick strands of shining
silver,
and thick blue cords trace,
on the backs of your hands, the curves of your calves,
messages of capability
learned,
practice,
passed on.

Then your flower,
in hues less livid, more subtly sensuous than now,
will focus all attention
upon the pearl of pleasure
it still enfolds.
And you will know
the heady woman-ness distilled in that crimson orb,
in which the flower is rooted still.
That orb,
grown solid, then,
small and strong,
withholds its living blood,
and in satisfaction
contains
the concentration of woman self-fulfilled.

For Alice... And For Me...

It is so much like being pregnant –
this being thirty-two
(and a half)
and dying.

So much like the pregnancy
which has frightened
and fascinated me,
and which I have avoided.

Death is like birth
and the awareness of your/my dying
is like the knowledge
of conception
within me.

Within my body it will happen,
sometime,
when the time is right.

And what will happen to me?
And what will I do?
And will it hurt?
Probably.

Untitled

We drove by today,
in as-it-is-now,
and,
as we sped past,
I turned my head to see
as-it-used-to-be.

But it was gone.
They tore it down.

the yellow farm house
with lilac bushes reaching second story windows.
The white-shuttered, yellow farm house,
shaded by two foot thick oaks,
standing in knee-high, gone-to-seed grass.

It was there just two weeks ago,
boarded-up windows enclosing with respectful decency
memories of strawberries hulled in the kitchen,
and Sunday chicken dinners with too many people
for the silverware that matched,
but the gravy was good.

There's a pile of coal there now.

There is No "Away"

Dead roses, petals of rust
that one week were gold
Something – was it once corn chowder?
has turned to penicillin
in its cottage cheese container
pushed to the back of the fridge.

A band-aid,
one drop of blood dried on its pad
from yesterday's tests
to see if my cancer is behaving itself.
Two empty plastic coated cardboard boxes
from macaroni and cheese,
Stouffer's does comfort food better than I do.
A plastic water bottle.
The empty can
from flat black spray paint
I used on that rocking chair.
A whole paper bag of crumpled Kleenex
from last week's head cold,
removed today from beside the bed.

In a city,
these would leave my awareness
as they left my hand,
fingers opening above the garbage can.

Here, in this tiny Appalachian hollow,
the roses,
the tissues,
the anonymous soup
go to the compost pile.
I carry that icky mess toward it
on the first step toward their metamorphosis
back into nourishing earth.

Water bottle and cottage cheese carton
rinsed into the red bin
Someday they'll make up a strand of yarn
in the fleece top of a rock climber
rappelling down a stony face.

I mourn briefly for the band aid and freezer boxes
as I throw them into the big black bag,
barred from the leavening cycles of life.

They'll live forever in a landfill
doomed never to rejoin the rest of us.

Even here in these woods,
I can't make everything all right.

The Master of Winnie-The-Pooh

You are washed, now,
and your hair is cut,
and your dog is bathed.
You have a plan for the future,
a car,
and a short-haired girl.

Perhaps now the aloneness will stay away.

As I smile at you,
I weep for you,
for we knew you were too special.
The world cannot bear such specialness,
and,
as we predicted,
you have died young.

Mirrors

These men,
these men who make us crazy
with their flatulence and football,
their lack of logic,
their loud assertions
when gentle questions are our need,
these men
are flirted with by other women at the party,
and flirt back,
then turn to us and pinch our bottoms,
and despite a wrinkle, a slippage, a bulge
not present when first, long ago, we flirted with them,
reflect to us our beauty
in their eyes.

Mud on her boots,
hair wet and stringy with melting sleet,
little balls of gritty, grey snow
weighting the bottom of her jeaned legs,
hands chapped, cracked and red,
March leans into the messy, difficult task of
turning February into April.

Curious Pocket

I slide my fingers into that curious pocket –
curious even to me –
which says I am a woman.

It was created by an Asian or Middle Eastern Goddess
for her own pleasure.
No American,
content with store-bought beads and instant mashed potatoes,
could conceive,
invent,
appreciate
this subtle grotto of contrasting textures and temperatures.

Indeed,
it was coaxed into reality
through the imagination of one
who, by habit, drank fine wine,
and ate elegantly-seasoned dishes
made from foods chosen early in the morning,
fresh,
in the marketplace,
and shared, in the gloaming, by candlelight,
with friends and a lover
accustomed to wearing brocade.

Dazzling Dancers

we invent concepts –
scarlet, ochre, mauve, crimson –
to try and trap them

but these obstreperous October leaves
refuse to submit to words

they move in Monet motion
and laugh
their rustling rainbow scintillations

Separation

In selfishness
I left your mind alone
I left you
to find
Someone in myself
Whom I could only find
In surroundings not familiar

Breast Cancer

Oh,
child that I never had,
I am about to lose
the warm, sweet glands
whose tips you never sucked;
whose milk never flowed,
white and rich and warm,
to become your pearly bones,
your wispy, peach-like down,
soon glinting against your nape,
then over your shoulders in waves.

Your soft mouth never closed,
needing,
over my nipple,
sucking, sucking,
till my hormones flowed with my milk
and my womb did a dance so joyous
that I gasped in stunned fulfillment.

And oh,
how the men who were never your father
reveled in those mounds.
Pressed against them,
they knew, unknowing,
the peace of succor
outgrown at their weaning.

Sucking till the pink rosebuds
flowered in the hungering mouths,
they drank the milk of my moans,
and arose satisfied.
But now,
my breasts –
even the word sounds curved,
comforting,
comfortable –
flow with death,
not life,
and shall be removed.

I await the tears that shall flow
like mother's milk
to nourish my grief.

These Women

These women,
full of questions,
breathe wisebreath.

These women,
recognizing the sacred,
put sage into the bouquets upon their tables,
and weeds into the salads.

These women,
knowing nurture,
raise my spirit as they do their herbs,
gently,
coaxing shadowy seeds of
possibility
into sweet leaves reaching forward.

These women,
together,
sit in a circle and sip,
from earthenware bowls,
the peace of right livelihood;
these women.

Peter

He was the sanest of all of us,
Really.
Of course, we all expected something
weird of him,
Under the circumstances,
Or I did, at least.

And later, of course,
He looked wilder and wilder.
But that didn't mean anything,
Because he was busy adopting a whole new culture.
Intact.
Oh, he shouted at her a bit,
But not as much as you'd expect,
And he came to us for a breathing spell,
And because the old-fashioned German gentleman in him
wanted things to be done properly.
I suppose it was rather wearing for him
to have us around all the time,
waiting for a chance
to be understanding.

So he drowned his old dreamless life
with some loud music and friends
and soon he became what he seemed.

Flight Path

Roots or wings? Wings or roots?
Cumulus clouds or rubber boots?
To soar in the sky or trudge on the ground – an important
decision to which I'll be bound.

A warm house, a garden, a child or two,
a partner to share all the things that I do.
Or – flirtations by moonlight with bottles of wine,
and lovers attentive can also be mine.

I am young and beautiful,
tan and talented,
Shall I waste it?

I am mortal, nothing lasts,
all is transient.
Can I ignore that?

Must life be either-or?
Must I choose
which to lose,
and which I must ignore?

I want it all. I'll have it all.
Upon the Muse of Life I call
to help me make my life a flight
of fantasy through air and light.

A flight which lands from time to time
in fields of grass with roots so fine
that though they hold the earth in form,
my fragile wings they'll not deform,
entwine, or forcibly hold,
but will form a soft nest,
when the sky grows cold.

Slippery

A smooth white ellipse of thought
slips erratically through my mind,
like a half-melted ice cube
sliding under my tongue,
not finding
an appropriately shaped niche
in which to stop.

Collective Conscience

Peace and wisdom
take shelter
in the night,
in candle-lighted living rooms,
and church basements,
their windows shedding golden light
upon shadowy shrubs.

We gather in safe and quiet covens
to share ideas:
love as wholeness;
the connectedness of all that is;
meaning in the patterns of
leaves,
shells,
children's minds;
ancient myths passed from mouth to ear,
changed
and unchangeable,
since before there was time.

Peace and wisdom
are sheltered
in the night,
behind golden windows.

Wife

"Do you know,"
she said one morning
as she finished coffee,
"I heard that there are
some call girls,
right here in this town!
And
they won't even look at
a man for less than fifty
dollars!"

After her husband
had left for work
she stood up and padded,
barefoot,
across the carpeted kitchen
to turn on the color T.V.

Renaissance

The tears of loss
drained my soul
without washing away its grief
The scald of nostrums
whitened my tumor away
and seared the blood from my womb.
I was dry
but I could not mourn the loss of my life's juices.
Parchment is dry;
it holds the wisdom of the ages.

The leaves of autumn are dry,
we celebrate their fall.
I settled into dryness,
rustled like a taffeta petticoat,
would not cry
for the sweet milk of youth
so suddenly gone.
I nested myself
in the whispering straw of age.
But you would not see dryness,
when you looked at me.
Your ears heard not
the crackling of dessicated lust.

And in me,
you touched what I could not feel.

Not the sweet watery nectar of spring,
the juice filled berries of youth,
but the clear syrups and thick red jams of harvest.

Sweet summer's flows come to fruition
and distilled, concentrated nourishment
for quiet, cold blue nights
that lead my soul, clean now,
bathed in rediscovered humors,
from the drought of its lonely losses
toward the shared crystalline rivulets
of spring thaw.

This Hospital

This hospital is
a sterile live trap for souls.
A beeping
traffic filled
hard lighted
unquiet
trap for souls struggling
in search of a zipper
of release
from this cocoon
of oblivious noise.

Leo

The clink of my spoon against the soup bowl
brings him down
from wherever he has cushioned himself
for this morning's long nap.
The fourteen years of our friendship
have only slightly muffled his perked ears.

Once again,
we have our familiar conversation
about the subtleties of feline and human table manners.
The repetition gives comfort to us both.
We polish our habits upon one another.

He leaps into my lap
and I bury my face in his ebony coat,
grizzled now,
with dignity and wisdom.

Between us,
knowledge of his magic lies, unhidden,
quiet,
both of us aware that it is there when we need it.
Was there when I needed him to tell Priscilla to come home,
after she had pouted two weeks in the woods
about the five days of cat sitter.

Was there the day Dave's cat was killed
and Schwartz knew he needed warmth
and purring beneath his chin
to help him believe in love again.

Today
with December wind blowing white crystals
stinging across crusted snow,
and frozen brown patches of earth,
my nose against his fur detects
from the sunny garden in which he curled in his dreams,
only just now ended by the sound of my lunch
the scent of roses in full bloom.

The Third of August

Three hours,
and a hundred and fifty miles
away from you.

The smell of our mingled sweat
on the skin of my shoulder
makes me want you
again.

Leave Him

I have watched, silent,
for several minutes
before I say softly,
"You are safe, here in our hollow."
The fox pricks forward her dark ears,
peers at me through a veil of green-budded foliage,
does not run.

We return to sunning ourselves,
introduced, now, to one another,
I on the grassy trail behind our house,
she on the bank beside the dry run,
separated only by three fragile apple saplings.
I press my face against the April sun,
as aware of her vulpine presence as she is of my human one.
She roots a bit in crackling leaves,
stretches, lies down,
licks a paw.
A tinge of red rusts her silvery fur.
Together,
we bask in the warmth,
the lacey verdure
finally replacing winter's gritty grey.

The fox alerts,
points her ears and muzzle in full attention,
as one of our cats wanders up the trail.

"No," I say quietly, firmly,
"you can't eat our cats."
She turns the triangle of her face to me,
eyes attentive,
studies me long,
stands and trots away.

Her den is here,
our back yard shared.
I have heard her often in the night,
yawping.
I know she will not go far.

As the leaves turned color last autumn,
while I was having my breasts removed to save my life,
Jimmycliff disappeared –
Jimmycliff the Rastafurian.

Each night, as I read in bed,
he had purred against my heart.
Each night he had crept beneath the covers,
and nestled his long black fur against my feet.

When I came home from the hospital
he was gone:
not dead and stiff beside our country road,
said my husband.
He had searched for miles.

Effective Advice

Tomato juice is not good!
It's a rural legend,
a fallacy.
Pour it on by the gallon.
Rub it in.
All you'll get are spaghetti stains,
you and dog you came in with,
will still smell of mercaptan.

Once I found out
that the guys hired to live trap skunks
for suburbanites
who want lawns that look like imitation grass,
and can't abide the burrowings of small animals,
fresh and clean
from the nests of their mammas,
looking to eat subterranean yellow jackets
who burst forth and savage playing grandchildren;
once I found out that those guys,
paid to disrupt the balance between creatures,
kill the skunks lured into cages by a trail of marshmallows.

Once I found that out,
I began a rescuing rampage.
Skunks are gentle;
they spray only when terrified,
and genetically refuse to carry lethal weapons.

Three I retrieved from death row cells
a smelly old geezer,
and two half-grown babies,
whose presence you would never detect by scent.
And it was my fault when I got sprayed.
In a hurry that day,
I didn't follow my own protocols:
soothe and sing to the caged –
feed sweet morsels –
Skunks do not fly;
She was in terror
when I abruptly swung her cage into the air.
I had to throw away even my underwear.

But in our woods,
now waddle and nuzzle
three new small, shiny eyed,
curious,
peaceful
black and white creatures.

Ripening

Nearly forty…
two days more.
And I am pregnant
with myself.

Legacy

The mothers and the fathers
who bear children
can go, complacent, into that dark night,
knowing that the shape of their cheekbones,
the shade of their eyes,
the imprint of their hands,
will be carried into far off generations
by scion who have no way
to shrug off this duty.

I am one who has no sons or daughters.
What immortality I shall have,
is not the unavoidable command of blood,
but is fragilely spun of shared time,
shared thoughts,
shared laughter and mourning,
with nieces and nephews
made my heirs by decision, not fate.

We share no ancestors,
yet with my stories
I can give them mine.
We share no descendents,
unless they choose to carry what I offer
to the children of their own futures.

Wash Day

Coaxing wrinkled laundry
to smooth out
to fold
at sharp angles,
you sit contentedly
easing away hints of disarray
with wrinkled trembling fingers,
the spirited ramble of imperfection
flattened by your touch.

Was there ever space for whimsy
in your ordered world?

Now you say,
"I never tasted rutabagas before."
Your memory,
once the sharp creases
of an origami treasure box
is easing away the tiny wrinkles
and the truths of your past,
baring hints of disarray.

I sit,
sadly watching perfection fade
from your own innocent unfolding.

Desperate Measures

To keep me alive,
they say they must tear the warm, wet, pink places out of me.
No, not tear,
burn them to dry dust.

Chemicals poured into my veins
sear out roundness,
heat,
moisture,
from soft places that have always provided
the nurture,
the pleasure,
the energy,
for my thought and my words.

Parts of me –
my mind, my body, my self –
that once were curved
are beginning to shrivel into flatness;
flat words,
flat thoughts,
flat breasts;
no contour to my sense of who I am,
just dry,
flat plains.

Between my thighs,
the soft, damp garden that once connected
my brain to my typewriter,
my love to my lust,
dries,
shrivels.
Burned by chemicals,
it not longer blossoms with velvety, crimson orgasms,
lusty, purple lyrics
or trembling, lavender haiku.

Its desiccated leaves crackle when I walk.

Willie

There's a hole in the fabric of the universe
where you went through.

We'll mend it up
with multicolored patches of love,
but under the iridescent stitches made of tears,
there will always be
a hole in the fabric of the universe.

Reconstellation

The diamonds that my mother wore,
and my grandmother, and my aunt –
tiny, some of them – are no longer held within the circlets of gold
that sealed their days
to the men with whom they shared their lives.
Now,
reset, they are combined
and flash rainbow patterns
across the days of my life.

My great-grandmother's butter dish was silver,
its feet filigreed,
a serene, sculpted cow
the handle of its domed lid.
At each Christmas and birthday of my childhood,
it offered its golden bounty
from the center of my grandmother's lace tablecloth.
Now,
as we light the candles on my niece's cake,
it gleams from the china closet in my brother's dining room.

In the barn behind his house
are lawn mowers, rakes, jugs of motor oil.
It smells as my father's garage did all my life.
And now,
on the workbench taken from that garage,

are little metal cabinets
with tiny, sliding drawers,
labeled in my father's hand:
"1/2" washers,"
"woodscrews,"
"machine bolts."

For years
the black, etched-glass vase
sat on a round mirror on my grandmother's table,
first thing you saw, coming in the front door.
After that house was closed,
my mother put it on the shelf beneath our kitchen windows –
where I saw it, coming in the back door from school, each day.
Now, as we fill ourselves with turkey, sweet potatoes, cranberries,
that vase reflects candlelight
from all three of the tables we have fit, somehow,
into our dining room,
six hundred miles
and a half century
from my childhood.

Reconstellated,
these shining fragments of others' lives
form a drinking gourd for me to follow as now,
I now walk an unmarked path
through my own.

White Flags

Three does,
four – look!
a scintillation of leaves upon a horizontal shadow
reveals a fifth drift into sight
beneath the wild crab apples at the edge of our clearing.

Usually, Charley's big, black presence,
his "Ah-roooo!" bark,
keeps them deeper in the woods.
But in the week since my neighbor took up pot-shotting
if my hens and roosters chicken-walk down the lane,
into her yard,
I lock the screen door at bedtime,
for gentle Charley knows how to turn the knob
and go into that dark night.
Can the deer know this in so few days?

A doe steps clear of October's jewel colors.
She's darker than the others,
though all are greying with autumn,
her coat nearly black with rain,
more than usual white on her muzzle.
Does that mean the same in deer as it does in dogs?
On ballerina legs, two smaller ones join her.
April's fawns, so tall in fall?

The deer chew and drift,
chew and drift.
A few of my soggy-plumed chickens
scratch in the wet, wet leaves
between their tiny feet.
I slide, noiseless, out onto the porch,
begin to chant.
Five heads rise.
Tails flag white.
the deer stare.
Softly,
I chant.

First the large, dark doe,
then the others as one,
as autumn drizzles,
lower their mouths to the ground,
resume savoring juice from tiny apples.

Roses in the Sun

I hold my arms around you,
my face pressed to your hair,
your face against my neck.

I have never been so alone.
I have never been so with you –
even in love making, never so intensely with.
I have never been so married.
I have never been so alone.
I have never been so with.

I know what is to happen,
so I have put drops of rose attar on my neck,
on the pulses in my neck.

I whisper frantically, calmly,
"John we're doin' it!
This is what being married means.
This is the sickness part of 'in sickness and in health.'
This is the worse part of 'for better or for worse.'
We're doin' it John.
This is being married.
We're doing this together. I'm here."

I move my leg and nearly slide off your narrow hospital bed,
the sheet covers a slippery plastic mattress cover.

I've already turned off the hissing oxygen machine.
Even with it on,
your breathing is irregular,
but the green tubes bind your face to this place,
and I have removed them.
This is not a good place to die,
but neither of us is aware,
both of us burning
with these hard spasms of dying.

Yesterday, you followed me with your eyes
And tried to form the word "love"
when I whispered it to you.

Today,
I felt your muscles relax when first I held you.
But your gaze is fixed now.
I midwife your labor with my arms and my whispers.
"I smell roses in the sun, John, roses in the sun.
Can you smell them?"
I name animals who have loved us:
Pallie, Prima, Boots, Amber.

"Amber, John, I see Amber."
And I do.
I picture her heart-shaped face so clearly that
surely the image passes from my awareness into yours,
with your face so close to the pulses in my neck,
so close to roses in the sun.

Your last breath rounds your mouth to "O."
Your eyebrows rise.
What is the surprise John?
What have you found fascinating?

The pulse in your neck continues past your last breath.
I hold you till that pulse in your neck stops, too.
And sit a little while longer,
for I don't know how long it takes
a spirit to leave its body.

So I sit a little while longer.

Life does not cease to be funny when people die, any more than it ceases to be serious when people laugh. – George Bernard Shaw

We file,
a whole town of us, it seems,
into our seats upon
sweetly worn, old oak pews.

Georgi, a family member by all
but the tiny twists of protein
unseen within the
rich, wet, centers of her cells,
has been asked to sit with the relatives.

When the church has filled to standing room,
they are escorted, pulling off dark gloves,
on this cold, late winter morning,
into the front rows.

Georgi, too,
has dressed in black and gray
for this mourning.
but, swinging with each step,
a fur muff hangs from her right wrist,
against the cold wind of the coming graveyard.

It took G. B. S., the succinct, salty old sage,
twenty-one words to say this.

Ursa Major

When I flip on the outside light,
the bear is sitting on his haunches,
like a cat,
beside the back porch.

It isn't a complete surprise:
when Charley wakened me,
racing between back door and stairway,
he wasn't saying "wuf-wuf."
His ancient wolf blood was howling "Ah-roo! Ah-roooo!"

The galvanized, five gallon garbage can,
with a bail to lock its cover,
is on its side,
handle ripped off, bail jimmied,
chicken feed strewed across the floorboards.

Presumably,
pleased with himself,
the bear sits, comfortably slumped,
chewing,
reaching a paw,
now and then, beneath the porch rail,
to swat another swath of grain
into eating distance.

Side by side,
Charley and I watch through the latched storm door.
Finally,
I rap against the glass and call,
"Go away, Bear, go away!"
emphasizing the capital letter of his name.

Bear jerks his head upward from his feast,
stands, turns, and
between a walk and a lope,
heads toward the woods.
Thirty feet or so from the porch,
Bear stoops to look over his shoulder:
"Go away, Bear," I call again, rapping on the glass.
This time, Bear chooses a definite lope
into the woods.

Since then,
a couple of people have asked,
"Was it a big bear?"

"All bears are big,
at three in the morning,"
I reply.

Treads

When I wear my mary janes:
    I used to feel silly,
    Till I found their soles are slippery.
    And now I slide, and whirl and turn
    And tap and dance.
    I feel as graceful as a golden leaf
    Twirling in the blue
    October sky.

When I wear my cowgirl boots:
    I stride, with long steps,
    Clunking my heels,
    And everyone can hear me coming.
    I feel ready for adventure,
    As strong and brave
    as a cowgirl, rescuing a lost calf.

When I wear my flip flops:
    I wiggle my toes
    And flap about like a baby duck
    On his way to the water.
    I feel as happy
    As if I were
    Playing in the waves
    On a soft, sandy beach.

When I wear my bedroom slippers:
    I walk soft and even my thoughts
    Are whispers in my head.
    My feet are gentle to the floor.
    I feel quiet,
    and glad my toes are being cuddled warm
    and glad for my safe and cozy bed.

When I wear my sneaks:
    I leap and arch and slam dunk
    every imaginary shot.
    I am graceful as a panther;
    I run on air.
    I feel like a sweaty heroine
    sent in to win the game
    at the very last moment.

Glorious

Yellow-red cherry
plucked in happy eagerness
draws forth mouth juices

Cues

For Homer, nothing smaller than decades of battle
between nation states
was worthy of epic verse

Yeats believed that real life took place one spring day in the
Dublin post office, 1916.
though he did pour a little ink
upon the moon dance of a cat.

But a feral poem rests gently on my bedspread this morning,
when I wake to see a beam of sun
in the fur of the grey mama cat
purring patiently beside me.

And surely,
my mother's blue veined hand
wearing her wedding ring,
securely and surprisingly attached to my own wrist,
is a silent sonnet.

There is rhyme riding on the back of the dog
whose sweet fur smells as it did when he came to me
a dancing pup;
the dog with cloudy eyes who trusts me
to help him up the porch steps
after our short, slow walk.

A villanelle lies among the bills,
another in the blue envelope with Amy's address in the corner,
and on the refrigerator, another,
in Molly's drawing of a bunny

A free, open unpredictable verse nestles
in the soft, hand-woven scarf he bought me.
It warms my chest
as I leave in the half-awake morning,
after a night when we have slept apart, in anger.

Early Morning

I savor
the slow, secret, silvery seconds
before others awaken.

Pillowing, velvet-scented coffee stream
connects me to the quiet kitchen,
as I listen in sensual silence
to the wakening dawn.

And,
as it cannot,
once it grows into a full and busy day,
the drowsy, loving morning listens to me.

On the Sundering of the World Trade Towers and the Pentagon

So strong we are,
so free
to drive, to fly.
We try to practice humility…
we try.

When we have time,
We help others climb
to stand beside us, strong and free…
when we have time.

The Tutsis have too far to climb –
we don't have time.
And three quarters of a million are machete'ed into the past
of a raw and oozing country.
We drive fast.

And the Palestinians and Israelis –
bad, bad children
of the same God in different hats –
they are quite too much to handle.
As they blow each others guts out
in sibling rivalry,
we soar our skies, and roll along our interstates.

But now,
someone weak and crazy mean,
mean with the evil spite of the overlooked,
has learned to fly.

In a suburban bedroom,
a young father in Italian loafers
weeps into the wispy, transparent hair
of a toddler calling, "Mommy!"

But Mommy now is chunks of meat,
the golden ring of promise still encircling
a grey-dusted tube, once her finger,
flattened yesterday,
with a fiery, metallic, shrieking sound,
beneath a fractured steel beam.

Now there is no place to drive,
to fly.

We huddle close to the ground.

My War on Terror, 2001

Another hen is gone this morning--
"Feet," who began as "Fancy Feet," when she hatched with
fluffy feather boots.
Since her pipping in the summer,
anthrax has polluted our mailboxes and our vision of the future,
and three thousand families have wept into
broken concrete and ruptured steel
from two tall buildings stretching by cranes into the sky,
for the purpose of counting the world's money.

Here,
I go on proofing the laying box against predators,
rolling medicine up in peanut butter balls for a gut-sick goat,
bickering with the husband I love,
offering a plain and sturdy table –
Indoors or out, your choice – around which to sit together,
and ponder how to remain kind in a world full of fear.

My gift, an island of sanity,
of beloved Earth,
of well-fed birds,
of listened-to friends – feather fur and skin –
this is my gift,
the only one I can present with the excellence of crafting,
demanded
in a world awash in the caustic tides of terror.

There is a "We"

He'd once heard a buddy no one could get to
burn up in an upside down pickup truck.

My life thus far more gentle,
I keep the pockets of my purse
filled with crackers for goats.
A plastic kangaroo and chicken slide around
with the pennies and grit.
At the bottom of my purse,
and in a special pouch,
bandaids, Excedrin, throat lozenges,
and a mini pad or two.

In the back of my car
A big orange hippopotamus says "grunt"
on the case covering a prn pillow.
There is a "we"
an unnamed swath of humanity
who pays attention
to what they have learned
about being human,
about living in real time,
about how to make it better,
whatever IT may be.

My Goat's Got a Buzz On

Oh, my goat's got skinnier every day,
despite 16 hours of munching hay.
I got worried with all I saw;
soon all that's left of Addie would be her "Baaa!"

Chorus:
Oh, my goat's got a buzz on –
Yeah, she's got a real buzz on.
She drinks four bowls of beer a day, (in the kitchen)
just to help her to digest her hay.
She'll have four bowls again today.
Yeah my goat's got a buzz on!
She's got a big buzz!

Well, I talked to farmers, and I questioned friends,
scared of how the story might end.
I paid for tests – they came out OK,
but the goat got sicker every day.

(Chorus)

I cried and cried, said "Addie my love,
I've searched the Earth and heaven above,
but no new wisdom did I get."
So we got in the car and went back to the vet.

(Chorus)

The vet checked her out, said, "Addie Dear,
I think we'd better try you on some beer."
Back at home, I popped a top,
poured Addie a bowl, but then I stopped.

Drank the rest myself and had a good day,
and all the while, Addie munched on hay –
then came back for another bowl!
Hey! Maybe my goat was on a roll!

   (Instrumental interlude)

Now Addie bleats, "Fill that bowl real quick,
'cause I sure don't wanna get all sick."
We sit in the sun a couple hours a day,
while that little goat grins and munches hay.

   (Chorus)

Talking with Dead People
Sometime after 1995

Since her death,
my mother has spoken to me several times.
Twice in the shower –
"Ma, what are you doin' in here?" –
once at the gym;
the last time,
along with my aunt Paree, her sister,
in my hospital bed,
as though they had waited
for the surgeon's report before they spoke.

Was it a dream,
a reaction of warm, wet, orphaned brain chemicals
as I rinsed shampoo from my eyes;
as sweat soaked my gym clothes,
as I swam upward in pain
through the nausea of anesthetic?

Four months after my mother died,
three of us,
three women,
Bib and Georgi and I
had a beach vacation at my parents' house.
"Hello,"
awakened Bib one night.

The tone was friendly,
that of a hostess.
Bib recognized my mother's voice
and went peacefully back to sleep.

Six years before my mother,
my father died
He hasn't said a word to me since.
But then,
we never had much to say to one another
except when we argued.

Honest to a Fault

Yawning is wonderful,
like surfing.
Sliding down that yawn…
    "Do you mind
      if I plagiarize that?
      I'll footnote it.
      You can number the footnote,
      if you wish,
      since you're supposed to.
      Ok.
      I'll plagiarize the number, too.
      I think I'll make it ten."

Reflexive Instincts

The cat
rolls over and exposes his ivory,
middle-class cat paunch to be rubbed,
curls and uncurls his brown velvet paws,
purrs a wheezy crescendo.

He rights himself,
moves in a languorous waddle
to meow at the door.

Outside, he moves slowly across the lawn,
stops to stretch,
and then…
his pupils contract to black periods in a sea of azure.

The slack muscles contract.
The rushing blood heats his thick, chocolate ears.

He stalks.
He pounces.

Ripping with rapid thrusts of extended back claws,
sinking long canines into soft, red flesh,
he tears the fur, the skin,
from the side of an adolescent rabbit
tasting the greenness of summer.

He leaves it
with its unfocused eyes rolling wide,
its blood oozing onto the ground,
as it crawls toward leafy cover
through grass
over which it bounded a few minutes ago,
with unconscious animal delight
in its own existence and hard muscles.

The cat sleeps, curled into a comma,
on the sheepskin
covering the rocking chair.

Roadway trailer truck
mystic industrial roar
of hydrocarbon contentment

Casual Affair

"Now, whaja wanna go an' do that for?"

"Do what?"

"Go an' fall in love an' ruin a perfectly good romance!"

"I'm sorry. I din mean to ruin it! My tongue jus' slipped."

"Your wha??"

"My tongue slipped. I had it firmly tucked in my cheek – that's where I usually carry it – but one day it jus' slipped out, and I couldn't get it back in place."

"Well, you should be more careful.
Now I'm gonna have to get rid of the whole thing."

"Do you have to get rid of it? I rather like being in love."

"Well, it's jus' not done. You went and ruined it, an' now I have to scrap it!

"Phoo!"

Fresh

Finally,
in this June as brown as August,
the rain comes.

We stand beneath benevolent clouds
till our skins run with water,
then sit on the porch eating salad
at a blue, checkered tablecloth.

Silently,
warily,
a spike buck,
orange –
Oh! So very orange! –
against wet, green forest,
glides into the yard,
scans,
relaxes,
drops his head,
begins to graze.

Smooth, young,
he is wet backed and hard muscled,
as his coat runs with water,
and he mouths his green meal.

Concrete Abstractness

It seems,
sometimes,
that I spend more time than I really care to
in the fissure between the hemispheres of my cerebrum.
Unable to scale
the precisely-positioned,
incrementally-spaced
mental toe holds of the left wall,
or to rise
with unconscious energy
   (understanding that understanding "rising"
   is equivalent to, and a necessary prerequisite of rising),
to the convoluted, elevated,
right surface.

Trapped between
steep,
smooth,
wet,
oyster-grey walls,
I wear galoshes to keep cerebral-spinal fluid
from wetting my feet.

I do not catch cold.
I do not soar.

Edge Dweller

Like the deer, I am a forest edge creature.
Dappled shadow, where sun and dancing leaves meet,
is where I thrive:
I can see the horizon here, yet take shelter.
But deer are better than I at surviving.

I'd not be able to sustain myself in health,
in the hybridized landscape
of a mental suburb,
as they do,
with no loss of cervid grace,
reviled by householders who live in rows,
who forget that leaf eaters walking crooked paths
were there first,
as we forget the snake brain
underlying each memo and ballad.

And in the winter of a forest deep in shade,
no spotted fawn emerges from me,
to dance upon ballerina legs,
as I struggle to sustain life
upon stringy bark and rotted acorns
pawed up from the mildewed duff of my soul.

Yet, like the deer,
my home is where edges meet.

Advancing

How often I've wished not to have to be the oldest one;
the one to test the waters,
break the trail,
show everyone else how to breast life's stages and storms,
crest them,
and go on, feathers flying,
with looser skin
and tighter logic.

But no,
perhaps it is not always so.
Sometimes, I am not the one to lead.

Lana cares for her mother,
changes her diaper,
feeds her with a spoon,
gets up in the night to comfort the confused cries
of Stella's
tired,
damaged
old brain.

Denise, my old roommate the artist,
pretty always,
beautiful now, at forty,
with long, golden hair,
a husband and a two-year old,

has no time to mourn her mother –
dead these six months –
but for the care of a toddler,
the teaching of a course,
the work in her husband's business.

Ungrieved,
that lost love binds,
not in gentle folds
of sweet connection to that which was,
but with painful bands of guilt,
of loneliness unexamined,
chafing abrasions into her soul.

Colletta is sixty-five.
I'm older, now, than when she was, twenty years ago
when we met, and I came under her mentorship.
In a few days I will see her,
for the first time as a widow,
returned now
to the farm that was her home,
and mine,
and that of so many others.
Together with those old friends,
visiting as I am, for the last time,
we will make the farm ready to sell.

Sixty-five, widowed, wistful,
optimistic, guilty, accepting,
Colletta is thinking of starting a business in Houston.

She will help young people find scholarships.
And I shall plant a Stella cherry tree,
for Lana, when she is orphaned.
And send a poem to Denise.
Perhaps it will stir,
from her,
a piece of art.
And we shall be less lonely,
the three of us.

Younger than I,
Lana and Denise let me watch
the pains of their labor,
as they struggle, to give birth to themselves,
to separate forever from the mothers who first bore them.

And Colletta,
seventeen years my senior,
and still nurturing for a living,
will show me how to walk away from our shared hearth,
leaving,
not her soul,
but only a few drops of drying blood.

Cocoon

Through an open window,
the wingtip of autumn
brushes my cheek in the night.

Without wakening,
I sigh,
and burrow sweetly
into my mounded cloud of flannel and feathers.

A lady in a straw hat and flowered dress
sits in an oak pew
with her mind folded

Helmsman

And now
I am in the front,
at the bow,
alone.

And sometimes,
when it is warm
the soft breeze,
no longer blocked by you who greeted it first,
feels like a caress on my skin,
on my face.

But when a cold and brutal wind
stings tears from my eyes,
I remember that storms used to be fun –
like the fear on an amusement park ride –
when you were in the front,
at the bow,
to shield me from blustery gales.

Of course, of late,
I have had to hold you up
in your position in the front,
at the bow.
It took much of my energy,
but even then,
it was you who went first,

as I remembered how you held me,
so long ago,
when we crossed the dangerous road.

For a long time now,
my children, my protégés,
have stood behind me
as I shielded them from my position
behind you
in the front,
at the bow.

But always it was you who went first,
as the cutting wind
left its signature of wrinkles
upon your exposed face.

And now, you have slipped off,
into the quiet deep, inhabited by so many others
whose snapshots are on my desk
and in my head.

And I am in the front,
at the bow,
alone,
cutting through the wind
with my children, my protégés,
behind me.

Words for my Funeral

I grew up in woods with animals, with birds singing, with cats;
I shall grow old and die in woods with animals with birds singing,
with cats.

I have danced and sung and cooked and fed my friends,
And flirted and cried and talked and written and danced
and loved.

Always I have loved, sometimes unwisely;
Sometimes with a lack of awareness akin to cruelty;
Sometimes as a martyr,
But mostly joyfully –
And yes, I have loved myself.

I have loved the women in my life –
my mother, Paree, the young girls with whom I shared a dorm
and an adolescence, Colletta, Laurel, Jewel, Lana, Georgi, Bib.
And the men: Trev, Ken, Ed, Larry, Willie, and so many lovers –
too many lovers? No, enough lovers to know love – and finally,
John, who will be a poem in the incense-scented bedroom of
my soul
long after we both shall be dead.

And he will be lucky if he doesn't die at my hand,
he so provokes me!

I part with all in sorrow and curiosity.

The best epitaph I've come up with, so far...

Surround her,
in your memory,
with leaves and creatures,
tears and flowers,
champagne and dancing.

Remember
the peace of solitude,
and of shared laughter:
a sufficient immortality.

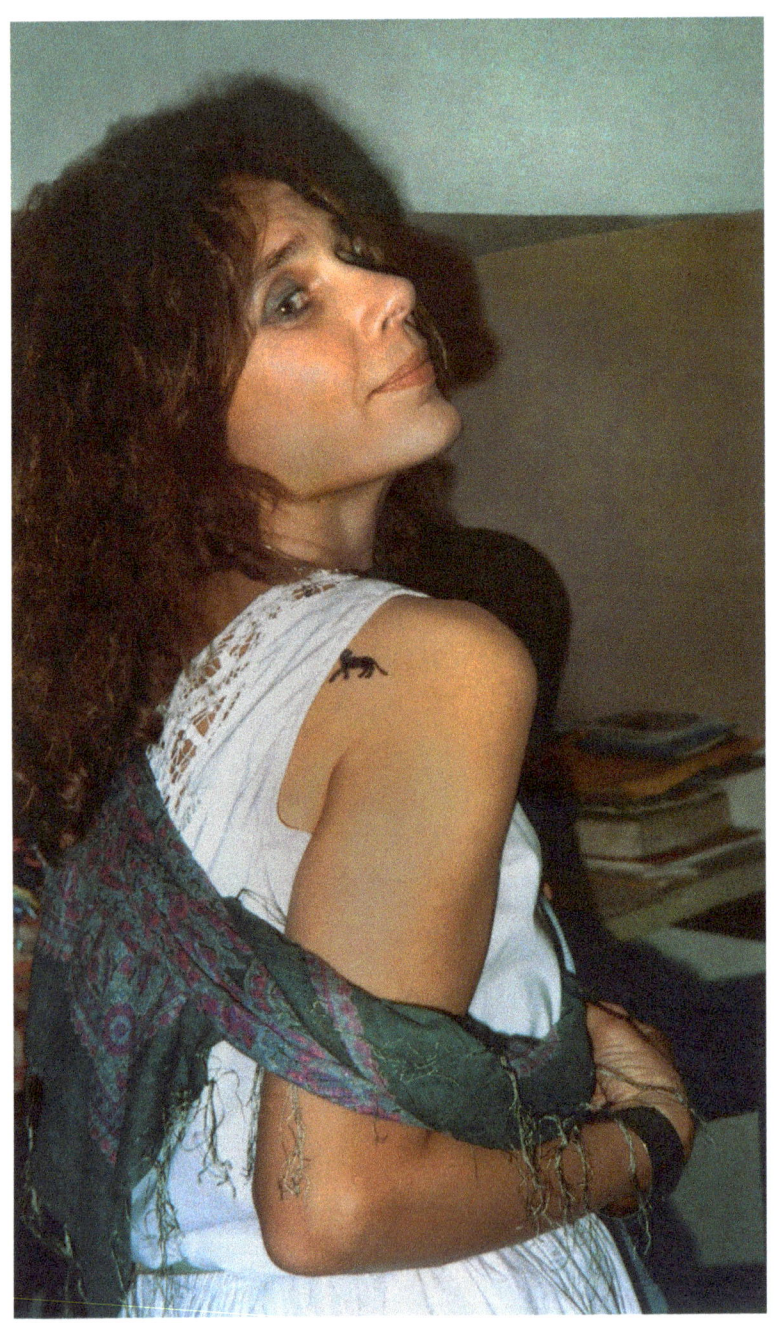

About the Poet

Born Corene Trevelyn Johnston in 1943 in Muskegon, Michigan, the poet had a traditional mid-western upbringing that nurtured her intimate connection to nature and her love for animals. Her poetry is autobiographical to a great extent, serving as a supplement to her lifelong passion for journaling. Corene valued formal education as demonstrated by her careers as a registered nurse, a nurse practitioner in Women's Health and a Reiki practitioner. She also believed that learning from alternative sources was as important as collecting degrees.

In addition to poetry, Corene wrote food articles, the "hard news" of a small town and a regular rural-life column for local newspapers and publications. Corene shared her life not only with her partners but also with numerous friends who she embraced as family.

Although she survived five episodes of breast cancer, she never allowed cancer to define her. Instead, she used this as yet another life event that influenced and focused her writing.

Corene left this earth in 2010, leaving behind family and friends who love her still for the precious gifts of love, laughter, spirited discourse and celebration of life.

Blessed Be and champagne all around.

Our soft footfalls on sodden leaves
becoming silence
as we stop to listen.

www.ingramcontent.com/pod-product-compliance
Lightning Source LLC
Chambersburg PA
CBHW040334300426
44113CB00021B/2745